Death and Immortality

D. Z. PHILLIPS

Senior Lecturer in Philosophy
University College of Swansea

Macmillan
St Martin's Press

First published 1970 by
MACMILLAN AND CO LTD
London and Basingstoke
Associated companies in New York Toronto
Dublin Melbourne Johannesburg and Madras

Library of Congress catalog card no. 71-124953

SBN 333 10270 3

Printed in Great Britain by
ROBERT MACLEHOSE AND CO LTD
The University Press, Glasgow

For what are three-score years and ten compared with all eternity?

A. G. N. Flew

Eternity, on the other hand, never counts.

Søren Kierkegaard

To Monica

Contents

Editor's Preface

This series of 'New Studies in the Philosophy of Religion' is designed to interest a wide readership. Each monograph in the series deals with some of the questions which must occur to any intelligent person who reflects about religion. Those who are studying philosophy at university or college will find that the series as a whole covers all the main problems which a modern course in the philosophy of religion comprises. And professional philosophers will be interested in the many original, sometimes controversial, points which the authors of this series make in their several contributions.

Mr Phillips's study typifies this breadth of interest. Is death the end? Are men immortal? These questions are central for anyone who is trying to make up his mind about religion. They have engaged the attention of philosophers from Plato to Wittgenstein. Mr Phillips goes to the root of the matter when he insists upon considering what such questions *mean*. He reviews the opinions of representative philosophers, both ancient and modern, as to their meaning and argues forthrightly that many modern philosophers at any rate have misunderstood these questions. His principal targets for criticism are Professors Geach and Flew. Turning from apologetics, whether for or against religion, to the significance which he takes belief in immortality to have within religious devotion or discipleship, the author of this monograph develops with characteristic vivacity his own provocative account of what it means to say that death is not the end and men are immortal.

University of Exeter   W. D. Hudson

Preface

When the Editor of this series asked me to contribute an essay on *Death and Immortality*, he asked me to keep two things in mind in writing it. First, the essays in this series are meant to give readers some idea of work being done in the respective areas of investigation. Second, the essays are meant to be more than surveys of philosophical literature, and to present the argued point of view of the authors. In this essay, I have made the second point my main aim. In doing so, however, I have woven contemporary contributions to ethics and the philosophy of religion into the argument whenever a suitable opportunity arose. I hope that the references to and the quotations from other people's work do not affect the continuity of the essay unduly. Having chosen this context for such references, it was inevitable that no mention would be made of many philosophers working on these problems. This does not mean that I consider their work to be of less importance than that of the people I discuss. It will be noted that some philosophers provoke a rather fierce reaction from me. Nevertheless, I owe them a special debt of gratitude for the stimulus they provided me in writing this essay.

In the first chapter, I simply note without a great deal of discussion some logical objections to various suggestions about the possibility of survival after death. The notions of the survival of non-material bodies, disembodied spirits or new bodies, after death, all seem open to fatal logical objections. The crucial question is whether such notions are, as some have thought, necessary presuppositions of any kind of belief in the immortality of the soul.

In the second chapter, I argue against the view that immortality, understood as survival after death, and the notion of divine providence, provide the only rational satisfactory answer to the question, 'Why should I be good?' I argue that immortality and providence so conceived illustrate the very antithesis of any kind of moral concern.

In the third chapter, I begin the positive task of discussing talk about the soul in what I take to be its natural setting. This setting has a lot in common with ethical considerations, but I also try to show why saying this is insufficient to explain the *religious* significance of belief in immortality. Finally, I try to show how the discussion can throw light on the notion of praying for the dead and of the dead praying for us.

In the fourth and final chapter, I consider in the light of the previous chapter what the notion of truth might mean in connection with belief in immortality. I try to answer some recent criticisms of the absolute character of religious beliefs which rely on the fact that people can lose their faith. I try to show how such loss of faith does not involve admitting the hypothetical character of religious beliefs, and I end by offering an alternative account of loss of faith in an individual's life and in the culture in which we live.

I have discussed the cluster of problems which are to be found in this essay over many years with innumerable people. The problems were problems for me long before I came to philosophy. I have found help in discussing them with philosophers, religious believers and non-believers. I wrote the first three chapters while conducting a Summer School at the University of Dalhousie during the summer of 1969. I had formed most of my ideas before then, but I am grateful to the many friends I made there for providing me with the necessary stimulus of interest and conversation which made me set down my thoughts on paper. Finally, I should like to thank my wife for the numerous discussions we have had on these topics and for typing the manuscript of the book.

Swansea   D. Z. Phillips
Christmas 1969

1 Does Belief in Immortality rest on a Mistake?

For most contemporary philosophers of religion, the question which serves as the title of this opening chapter is one of the most intelligible that can be asked. The answer given to the question is all-important. For the most part, I shall not question this assumption in this chapter. On the contrary, I shall accept it and observe where it takes us. I do not think that it takes us finally to anywhere of very great interest, although much that is of interest and importance must be mentioned en route.

Does belief in immortality rest on a mistake? Probably, most philosophers would want to say that the notion of immortality is either wholly or partially mistaken. But what kind of mistake is involved? This question is answered usually in terms of a critical exposure of what are taken to be essential presuppositions underlying the notion of immortality. These presuppositions refer to issues which are not necessarily religious: survival after death, the problem of personal identity, the relation between mind and body, the possibility of disembodied existence, and so on. It is such issues as these that one finds being given prominence in philosophical discussions of immortality. Many philosophers would say that this is as it should be, since whether the belief in immortality rests on a mistake or not depends, to a large extent, on whether the presuppositions of the belief are intelligible or true. There are threads of connection between the concept of immortality and these presuppositions. If enough of these threads are broken, the concept of immortality itself collapses.

Most philosophers, I think, would say that belief in the possibility of survival after death is a necessary precondition of any kind of belief in immortality. But although words can be uttered which *seem* to make sense, words found in such expressions as 'We shall meet again beyond the grave', the sense they seem to have evaporates on a closer examination. For how can we survive the dissolution of our bodies? If we hear that someone has survived an accident, we know what is meant. But if we hear that someone has survived his death, we do not know what to make of these words. The report of the crew of a torpedoed ship which divides them into 'dead' and 'survivors' presents a logically exclusive distinction. Every member of the crew must have died or survived, and no member of the crew could have died and survived. Of course, the newspaper reporter may have as his headline, 'Torpedo Crew Survive Encounter With Death', or 'Torpedo Crew Member Survives Death', and we do not think it nonsense. We understand that what he means by the first is that the crew have survived a situation where the expectation and likelihood of death were particularly high. We understand too that what he means by the second is that a member of the crew who, because he showed all the customary symptoms, was thought to be dead, yet turned out not to be dead after all. In the light of such cases, however, we do not abandon 'we do not survive death' as a necessary truth. On the contrary, what we do is to introduce terms such as 'clinical death' to cover cases where, despite the presence of symptoms normally associated with death, the person may or may not survive (see [7]). (1) So the immediate problem facing someone who believes in immortality is to explain how it is possible for human beings to survive the dissolution of their bodies.

There are many ways in which this problem and its attendant difficulties have been met. One of these is to deny that the dissolution of our physical bodies is as crucial a factor as the denial of immortality supposes it to be. This might take the form of holding that when we die, what lives on is some kind of non-material body. Peter Geach has argued that the objections to such a view are empirical rather than logical. He says that 'the mind–body problem must after all be just the same for an ethereal body as for a gross one' ([9] p. 17). Philosophers, however, have a right to say something about the kind of conditions which must be satisfied if these non-material bodies are to be said to exist. If the believer in such bodies were to start qualifying his claim that they exist by saying that they did not affect any physical apparatus, or produce any physical effect at all, one would begin to wonder how the existence of non-material bodies differed from there being no such bodies at all. The notion of a non-material body would have died what Professor Flew has aptly called 'the death by a thousand qualifications' ([5] p. 97; cf. [9] p. 18). There is no alternative for those who do believe in the existence of non-material bodies but to agree that there should be some kind of evidence of their

2

existence. But when we look for such evidence we discover that it cannot be found. Geach asks with good reason,

> How is it, then, that 'subtle bodies' have never forced themselves upon the attention of physicists, as X-rays did, by spontaneous interference with physical apparatus? There are supposed to be a lot of 'subtle bodies' around, and physicists have a lot of delicate apparatus; yet physicists not engaged in psychical research are never bothered by the interference of 'subtle bodies'. In the circumstances I think it wholly irrational to believe in 'subtle bodies'. Moreover, when I who am no physicist am invited to study the evidence for 'subtle bodies', I find that very fact suspicious. The discoverers of X-rays and electrons did not appeal to the lay public, but to physicists, to study the evidence; and so long as physicists (at least in general) refuse to take 'subtle bodies' seriously, a study of evidence for them by a layman like myself would be a waste of time. ([9] p. 18)

It will be seen that anyone who construes immortality as the survival after death of some kind of non-material body is in considerable difficulty. If he denies the appropriateness of asking for certain evidence of the existence of such bodies, he unwittingly denies the logical propriety of his belief. If, on the other hand, he admits that the request for evidence is a proper one, he has to account for the complete absence of such evidence. (2)

It is true, however, that a believer in immortality may deny that the dissolution of the human body is a crucial obstacle to his belief, by other means. He may deny that his essence, his essential self, has anything to do with bodily existence at all, whether that bodily existence is thought of in material or non-material terms. He might say that his identity is to be found elsewhere. But where is it to be found? People who talk in this way are usually found to subscribe to a dualistic view of human beings. Human beings, it is said, are made up of two substances, one physical, the other mental. We call these respectively the body, and the mind or soul. The body, however, is not essential to what we mean by persons. It can be thought of as the prison within which the soul is temporarily restricted, the house within which it is lodged for a time, or as the suit of clothes which adorns a person for the moment. The essence of a person, what it means to be a person, is identifiable with the mind or soul. This being so, it is argued, it is not surprising that at the dissolution of the body, the mind or soul should continue to exist,

3

free at last from its former restrictions. It is all-important to this point of view to insist that 'I' can be identified with one's mind or soul. Thus, the departed souls really *are* the departed, not some mere remnant of them. If John Jones can be identified with his soul, then if John Jones's soul survives John Jones's death, John Jones has survived his death. Unless one's soul is oneself, its survival would be of no interest to one. As Flew says, 'The news of the immortality of my soul would be of no more concern to me than the news that my appendix would be preserved eternally in a bottle' ([4] p. 270).

Geach points out that one important source of the temptation to say that it is my mind that thinks, sees, hears, feels, etc., is the fact that words like 'pain' and 'seeing' can stand for private experiences. From the undeniable reality of such private experiences, some philosophers draw the fallacious conclusion that giving meaning to these words is itself a private experience. As Geach says, this conclusion 'is really nonsense: if a sentence I hear or utter contains the word "pain", do I help myself to grasp its sense by giving myself a pain? Might not this be, on the contrary, rather distracting? As Wittgenstein said, to think you get the concept of pain by having a pain is like thinking you get the concept of a minus quantity by running up an overdraft' ([9] p. 19). The point of Geach's arguments is not to deny that there are private experiences or to advance a behaviouristic thesis, although many will take him to be doing this, in the same way as they mistakenly thought Wittgenstein to be doing this before him. But, as Geach says, 'it is not a question of whether seeing is (sometimes) a private experience, but whether one can attach meaning to the verb "to see" by a private uncheckable performance; and this is what I maintain one cannot do to any word at all' ([9] p. 20). What then do we do when we give words a sense? Geach replies, 'We give words a sense – whether they are psychological words like "seeing" and "pain", or other words – by getting into a way of using them; and though a man can invent for himself a way of using a word, it must be a way that other people *could* follow – otherwise we are back to the idea of conferring meaning by a private uncheckable performance' ([9] p. 21).

Why does Geach want to stress so emphatically that giving meaning to words is essentially a public matter? In the present context, it is in order to free us from the picture of each individual enclosed in his own private world conferring on words his own private uncheckable meaning; a picture responsible for a long history of havoc in philosophy. If this picture is destroyed, the idea of the mind as the essentially thinking part of man is also destroyed. Geach points out that even in the case of words such as 'feel', 'see' or 'hear', we use them not solely to refer to our private experiences, but in connection with the physical characteristics of what is seen, heard or felt and the behaviour of people who see, hear and feel. These connections are not mere contingent features of the concepts concerned. As Geach points out, 'our ordinary talk about seeing would cease to be intelligible if there were cut out of it such expressions as "I can't see, it's too far off", "I caught his eye", "Don't look round", etc. Do not let the bogy of behaviourism scare you off observing these features; I am not asking you to believe that "to see" is itself a word for a kind of behaviour. But the concept of seeing can be maintained only because it has threads of connexion with these other non-psychological concepts; break enough threads, and the concept of seeing collapses' ([9] p. 21). Since these connections are not mere contingent features of the concepts involved, and since using such concepts is an essential part of the characteristic activities of persons, one cannot maintain that the essence of a person, what it means to be a person, has little to do with any of these things. The notion of the self is not the notion of an inner substance, necessarily private, whose existence and nature we must guess or infer from bodily behaviour which is but a pale reflection of the reality behind it. Persons are not mysterious entities that we never meet directly or have direct knowledge of. On the contrary, we do meet persons, come to know them to varying degrees, sometimes know them better than they know themselves, share or not share their private experiences, and so on. This does not mean that people are not often a mystery to each other, or that artists and writers were wrong in portraying situations in which the inner reality of people's thoughts is contrasted with the external façade of their lives. No, what is being said is that even these features of human existence depend on there being ways of life in which human beings share; on there being hopes and aspirations, longings and expectations, plans and disappointments, ways of working and playing, which people have in common. The problem is not one of discovering how to bridge an unbridgeable gulf between a number of logically private selves, contingently thrown together. On the contrary, unless there were a common life which people share, which they were taught and came to learn, there could be no notion of a person. To call these common activities a façade, an

5

outer show, and to contrast them with a logically private reality is a mistake, since without these activities there could be neither reality nor façade. What can sometimes be called a façade is a mode of life which stands in certain relations to these activities. To call these activities as such a façade, however, is to destroy the possibility of drawing any distinction between appearance and reality in this context. Furthermore, unless there were ways of doing things, common conceptual rules, which people share, people could not have experiences and thoughts, plans and desires, etc., which they do not share, but choose to keep to themselves. Our common ways of doing things are not generalisations from individual performances, but the preconditions of individuality. The public is the precondition of the private, not a construct of it. This being so, what it means to be a person cannot be divorced or abstracted from these common features of human life.

Thus, any attempt to say that the essence of the self is thought, and that this thinking self is best depicted as an inner substance, never directly knowable, is doomed to failure. Once this is admitted, the way of thinking about the immortality of the soul which goes along with this failure collapses. This way of thinking, you'll remember, suggested that the dissolution of the human body was not an insuperable difficulty for belief in the continuation of the self after death. Since the notion of the self has nothing to do with the body, or any external physical features of human existence, its continued existence can be maintained even in the absence of these external features. What we have seen, however, is that thought, said to be the essence of the self, so far from being unconnected or contingently linked with these so-called external features, is inextricably connected with them. The supposition, therefore, that something called a thinking substance could survive the disappearance or disconnection of these other features is fundamentally confused. A belief in the immortality of the soul which depends on such suppositions while thinking it has grasped the essence of the self has really grasped nothing at all. What I have tried to do is to ease open that grasp, since once it is opened, one can see that it contains nothing.

Before leaving this point, it is worth re-emphasising the main considerations connected with it. We have seen how tempting it is to equate the notion of a person with an inner thinking substance, the soul. This, it has been said, is what separates human beings from animals: the former possess souls while the latter do

6

not. Both men and animals perform physical processes, such as digestion, but only men perform thinking processes. Thus, the difference between men and animals is that the former have something extra going on *in* them. We have seen how misleading this way of thinking is. In the case of the physical processes, such as digestion, we can see that they do not depend for their meaning on the kind of life the human beings or animals lead. One can say that these processes fulfil their functions no matter what kind of life is led by the beings concerned. But one cannot say this of the host of activities we associate with thinking. (3) For example, this cannot be said of planning a car route. Unless the planning played a certain role in one's life, one would not call it planning at all. In the absence of such a role and of any explanation, such as that the person involved was joking, it would be of little use protesting that one was having an inner experience or pursuing an inner activity called 'planning a car route' all the same. Similarly, if one saw someone watering his garden every day, but then found out that he never planted anything in it, one would begin to wonder whether one could go on saying that he was watering his garden. But someone might ask why this should be so? Isn't the man who waters his garden without planting anything in it going through the same motions as someone watering the plants in his garden? Possibly. It might then be urged that since they are going through the same motions, they must be doing the same thing, but this does not follow. The reason, however, is not because the man who waters his plants has a mental image of a man watering his plants while the other does not, or because he has some kind of private experience which the other man does not have. On the contrary, in the two instances the reverse might be the case. Nevertheless, this would not lead us to say that the man who watered his garden without ever planting anything in it was thinking while the other was not. The essential difference between the two cases, what makes the one count as watering a garden and the other not, is the presence or absence of the role which watering a garden plays in the network of activities which goes along with this. When these contextual implications are absent, one is at a loss to know what the person concerned is doing.

Consider further the example of a carpenter who holds up different samples of window-frames to his eye, rejecting some and accepting others. Would we not say that he is thinking? Does he say anything? No. Does he have any mental images? He may deny this too. What makes us say he is thinking then? Surely, what

7

shows he is thinking is the connection between his acceptances and rejections and the rest of his day's work; it is this that shows one that he is thinking. The presence or absence of thought in this context depends on the reference to common criteria, the way the work is done; in this case, what counts as acceptance and rejection, etc. This means that whether the carpenter is thinking about his work or not cannot be settled by reference to what goes on inside him. What if the carpenter consistently accepted all the window-frames he should have rejected and someone says to him, 'You can't have been thinking about what you were doing', would it be of any use if he were to reply, 'Yes, I was thinking. I know I was because I observed a process going on in my mind'?

The reference to common criteria, to shared ways of doing things, in the above context, can be misleading. It may give the impression that whenever a man can be said to be thinking, he must be participating in an activity in which most or many men could share. This is not always the case, since the thoughts in question may be exceptional or original, in which case most or many people could not appreciate them. One might recall the story that Socrates once thought for twenty-four hours without moving. Here, there is no question of what all men do in such circumstances. What Socrates is said to have done depended very much on the kind of man he was, the extent of his dedication to philosophical enquiry, and so on. Nevertheless, this does not mean that there are no public criteria which enable us to say that Socrates had been thinking. These would be connected with what Socrates said later. What he said would be connected with his subject, and the originality of his remarks would be shown by the new difficulties he had seen, the puzzles he had resolved, the progress he had made, and so on. Of course, Socrates does not have to *say* he had made progress in order for this to be true, but it must be possible for him to say something about his thoughts if asked. It might be true that he had spoken to himself or had mental images, but these facts *in themselves* would not show that Socrates had been thinking. These facts would not be the distinguishing mark between Socrates's achievement and that of a cat which had not moved for twenty-four hours. How do we know that the cat is not wrestling with philosophical problems and that its contented purring is not a sign that a worrying puzzle has just been resolved? Might not the cat's silence be a sign of cussedness towards human beings? What right have we to say that the cat was not thinking for twenty-four hours? How are we

8

to know what went on within the cat? But once we ask this question we see that we are back with our old pseudo-problems. The point is that we can say that the cat has not been thinking, because the kind of connection with what went before and came after which we looked for in the case of Socrates plays no part here. Similarly, in the case of our first example, a chimpanzee may be trained to take down maps from a shelf and to run his finger along the lines which indicate possible car routes. Nevertheless, he is not planning a car route. The chimpanzee's movements are not linked to the rest of its life in the way in which planning a car route is linked to other activities and events in people's lives. It is important to remember that if chimpanzees do this kind of thing at all, it is usually behind bars in a zoo or as part of a circus act. They do not *use* the maps as human beings do. Their movements may be the same, but they do not have the same point. This is no trivial observation. On the contrary, it makes a world of difference.

Once again I wish to re-emphasise the dangerous misunderstandings that our discussion may lead to. These have been pointed out very well by Iris Murdoch (see [15]). There is a danger of developing Wittgenstein's attack on the notion of logical privacy in such a way that it leads to a disregard of the notion of 'the inner life'. Miss Murdoch finds indications of such a development in Stuart Hampshire's book, 'Thought and Action'. It is tempting to move from the correct observation that private experiences and thoughts are logically parasitic on public meanings, to the incorrect observation that it follows that private thoughts are somehow less real than public expressions. It is in this way that the proper attack on the notion of logical privacy can be extended improperly and result in a devaluing of the contemplative aspects of human life. Hampshire says, for example, that 'The play of the mind, free of any expression in audible speech or visible action is a reality, as the play of shadows is a reality. But any description of it is derived from the description of its natural expression in speech and action'. And again, 'The assent that takes place within the mind and in no process of communication when no question has been actually asked and answered is a shadowy assent and a shadowy act' (quoted in [15] pp. 345–6). But this way of talking is extremely misleading. A man may come to think of an acquaintance in a certain way after much heart-searching, reflection, consideration and rejection. Not all the thoughts that pass through his mind issue directly in word or deed, but that does not mean that they are any less important for that reason. The

9

analogy with the reality of shadows is extremely inappropriate. The shadow of a wall is dependent on there being a wall to throw the shadow; it is a one-way dependence. But this is not the case with thoughts which do not issue directly in expression or action. They can contribute indirectly in that they may involve the consideration and rejection of other actions or opinions which might have been given expression. But even when thoughts do not lead to actions or verbal expressions directly or indirectly, they may be extremely important. Iris Murdoch considers the case of a woman who, by reflecting on the life and character of her dead daughter-in-law comes to revise her whole conception of her. The person of whom she once thought unfavourably now appears to her in a most favourable light. There is no question of doing or saying anything about the changes brought about by contemplation, but who could deny their importance? What remains true and important is that such contemplation could not have taken place were it not for the fact that human beings are related to each other in certain ways, enter into relationships which often give rise to complex problems, and so on. Rush Rhees makes the same point when he says,

> I know that a man may be in love and not show it, either to her or to his friends. But I do not think he could be in love – and here I mean that I do not think it would make sense to say it of him – I do not think he could be in love and never do anything that would rightly be called an expression of it. If he does not show it to his friends, it will appear in his thoughts when he is alone. In the way and in the terms in which he thinks of her; and in the way and in the terms in which he thinks about the world now. None of this would be possible without language; and the lover's thoughts are in the language of love. ([26] p. 124)

Thus once again we can see that the attack on the notion of logical privacy is by no means an attack on the importance of what has often been called 'the inner life'. But by showing how the very possibility of such an inner life depends on there being activities and a language which people have in common, any attempt to identify the essence of the self with an inner substance divorced from such connections is shown to be radically confused.

So far, we have seen that difficulties arise for two attempts at construing the logic of the immortality of the soul. The first of these was the attempt to argue that by the immortality of the soul

10

we mean the survival after death of a non-material body. The second was the attempt to argue that by the immortality of the soul we mean the survival after death of a disembodied self.

We must now move on to a third difficulty. Even if we waived all the objections to the notion of disembodied survival which we have considered hitherto, the question would still remain regarding the identity of the person said to survive. Given the possibility of disembodied thoughts, *whose* thoughts would they be? It seems that in order to answer this question reference to bodily identity must be reintroduced. Geach points out that retrospective identification would not be satisfactory. One could not say that the thoughts were different because they once belonged to different bodies. He sees more hope if we agree with Aquinas that what makes them different is that they have a capacity for reunion with a body ([9] p. 23). But this means that the possibility of identification does depend on the possibility of men living after death as men. This brings us to the heart of the problem. Can men live after death as men?

One affirmative answer to this problem is given in terms of reincarnation: the departed soul lives again in a new body. Bernard Williams has discussed the possibility of Guy Fawkes living again in a man called Charles (see [37]). But these cases rest on taking memory-claims as a sufficient condition of personal identity. What are we to say if Charles can remember what we think only Guy Fawkes could have known? Williams points out that what happened to Charles could also happen to Robert. We should now have to say that both are Guy Fawkes. But this is impossible, since we should have to say that Guy Fawkes is in two places at the same time. We couldn't say one was Guy Fawkes and that the other was extremely like him, since we would have no criteria for making such a distinction. 'So', Williams concludes, 'it would be best, if anything, to say that both had mysteriously become like Guy Fawkes, clairvoyantly knew about him, or something like this. If this would be the best description of each of the two, why would it not be the best description of Charles if Charles alone were changed?' ([37] p. 239). Williams makes the extremely helpful suggestion that in such contexts 'same memories' should be understood as a claim of exact similarity, which is *not* a claim of identity. Williams says, 'The only case in which identity and exact similarity could be distinguished . . . is that of the body – "same body" and "exactly similar body" really do mark a difference. Thus I should claim that the omission of the body takes away all content from the idea of personal *identity*' ([37] p. 241). (4)

Thus, it seems, if a claim is to be borne out that so-and-so is so-and-so living again, it must be established that there is a one–one relation between the material bodies involved in the two spans of existence. As Geach points out, this one–one relation is central to our ordinary assertion that this old man is the same person as the baby who was born at such-and-such a time. It is not that the growth of the baby into an old man is observed, and thus taken as proof of identity, but that should any difference be established, it would be taken as disproving identity ([9] p. 26). Of course, it is not necessary that there should be material identity between the body of the baby and the body of the old man, or between the body of the man who lived and who now lives again. 'So', Geach concludes, 'the upshot of our whole argument is that unless a man comes to life again by ressurection he does not live again after death' ([9] p. 28). Geach says that it is hard to believe in the resurrection of the body, and he is certainly right about that, but he wants to say that it is even harder to believe in the survival of a soul whose very identity depends on its being reunited with one body rather than another, but which in fact is never so reunited. Geach also admits that there are no philosophical reasons for believing in the resurrection of the body, and that there are often strong empirical objections against such a belief. 'But', he concludes, 'apart from the *possibility* of resurrection, it seems to me a mere illusion to have any hope for life after death' ([9] p. 28).

Let us briefly retrace our steps. We have seen that there are grave difficulties in construing belief in the immortality of the soul as belief in the survival of a non-material body or the survival of a disembodied spirit after death. We therefore seem forced to say that the only possible way in which to understand the hope of immortality is to assert the possibility of the physical resurrection of the body after death. But this assertion brings with it its own crop of problems, since what *is* this possibility that we are being asked to entertain?

It seems that one assumption behind the claim that survival after death is a possibility is that death can be thought of as an event in one's life. Thus, one might ask whether one can survive death in much the same way as one might ask whether someone can survive in a room temperature of such-and-such degrees. In fearing death it seems that one is fearing an experience, something that is going to happen to us all. And, of course, something *is*

12

going to happen to us all: we are all going to die. But when we speak in the first person singular and say, 'I am going to die', we are saying something logically very different from saying, 'I am going to faint', or 'I am going to have an accident'. For death, if it is to be construed as an event, is always an event for spectators, never for participants. As Wittgenstein said, 'Death is not an event in life: we do not live to experience death' ([40] 6.4311). We are often told from pulpits that death is part of every man's experience, while the truth is that death is not part of any man's experience. One might be led to construe death as an event by failing to notice that one cannot say of one's own death what one can say of the deaths of other people. If one were asked what one meant by saying that so-and-so was dead, one might reply by saying that such-and-such organisms had ceased to function in him, that he died of certain ailments, that he will no longer be seen walking, talking, carrying on his business, etc. Here, death is spoken of in the third person. Death is an event in someone's world; an event of the greatest importance perhaps, or maybe an event of no importance at all. But when this death is *my* death, it is not an event in the world for me. And hence it is radically different from the thousands of events that happen to me – my toothache, my accident, my marriage, etc. etc. All these are events in my world, and although there are important differences between saying 'I am in pain' and 'He is in pain', 'I am in pain' means for me the same as what saying 'He is in pain', with reference to me, means to another person. Now it is true that there is much in common when I say 'I shall die soon' and when another person says of me 'He will die soon'. The kind of implications these statements have in common are similar to those indicated above. But the statement 'I shall die soon' cannot be analysed exclusively in these terms. My death is not an event in the world for me, but the end of the world. Death is not an experience, but the end of all experiences, and one cannot experience the end of experience. W. H. Poteat expresses this point well:

Just as Hamlet's question 'To be or not to be . . .' is logically not like 'To be or not to be a doctor, lawyer or merchant chief . . .', so contemplating the ending of my life is logically not like ending a job or a marriage. It is an end of *all* possibilities for something, namely, for what I name with the personal pronoun 'I', and not just the ending of certain possibilities such as this or that. We can say 'After his divorce he was remarried', or

13

'. . . he was sadder but wiser'. To go with the expression 'After he died . . .' there are no expressions logically like 'he remarried' or 'was sadder but wiser'. ([22] pp. 133–4)

But when we ask whether there is life after death we *do* seem to be wanting to follow the expression 'After he died' with expressions such as 'was sadder but wiser'.

Geach refers to Saint Paul's use of the simile of a seed that is planted and grows into an ear of corn, and suggests that this might illustrate the relation between the corpse and the body that rises again from the dead:

> This simile fits in well enough with our discussion. In this life, the bodily aspect of personal identity requires a one–one relationship and material continuity; one baby body grows into one old man's body by a continuous process. Now similarly there is a one–one relationship between the buried seed and the ear that grows out of it; one seed grows into one ear, one ear comes from one seed; and the ear of corn is materially continuous with the seed but need not have any material identity with it. ([9] p. 28)

Whatever spiritual truths can be derived from Saint Paul's simile, it cannot be seen as a suggestive simile in illustrating the possibility of the resurrection of the body from the dead. We can say 'After the seed is buried, an ear of corn grows out of it' only because, as Hume would no doubt point out, it is a process with which we are familiar. We can say that the buried seeds result in the growth of corn because such a process is known and is intelligible to us. But there is no such process which makes talk of buried corpses leading to new bodies rising from the dead intelligible to us. On the contrary, we know that this kind of thing does not happen. In the case of the buried seed, one could resolve the issue experimentally. If someone asks whether buried seed leads to the growth of plants he is asking a straightforward empirical question. But if one asks whether people live after death, is one asking a question of the same logical character?

At this point a philosophical and popular agnosticism is likely to be introduced into the argument. Someone is likely to say that we just do not know what happens to a human being after he dies. Our language, it might be said, is too confined to tell us anything about the world beyond the grave. This suggests that the question of life after death is a factual question, but that the conditions

14

necessary for the resolution of the question are unfortunately absent. But this popular philosophical response is based on misunderstanding. The question is not whether there is or there is not life after death, where affirmative or negative answers to the question would both be considered intelligible, possible answers, whether they were true or false. The question is whether it means anything to talk of life after death. If one understands what is meant by 'survival' and what is meant by 'death', then one is at a loss to know what it means to talk of surviving death. Thus, to say that our language is too confined to tell us anything about the world beyond the grave simply obscures the issue. First, if it is interpreted as meaning that we do not know the answer to a factual question it obscures the fact that unlike other factual questions, where we know what it *means* for the answers to them to be affirmative or negative, here we do not really know what is being asked. Second, if it is interpreted as meaning that our language *as such* is inadequate to tell us anything about the world beyond the grave, the notion of inadequacy is being misused. Our language is not a poor alternative to other means of communication; it is what constitutes communication. To say 'We only have our language', in this context, is not like saying 'I only have English'. In the latter case one might say, 'If you could speak Welsh you'd see why *hwyl* is untranslatable.' But one cannot say, 'Because we only have our language we cannot say what the world beyond the grave is like.' There can be an inadequate use of language, but it makes no sense to say that language itself is inadequate. One might be misled into thinking this by the use of such expressions as 'Words can't tell you how grateful I am'. Such sayings are misconstrued as inadequate expressions, whereas their actual use *is* to express great gratitude. That they are appropriate rather than inadequate expressions is shown by the fact that there are criteria for determining when it would be inappropriate to respond in that way, for example, in response to a trivial act of courtesy.

Of course, the above conclusions about language's adequacy and inadequacy do not imply that it is impossible to put words together in such a way that they seem to make sense even when they are in fact nonsensical. Such is the case when we speak of bodies rising from the dead. Suppose we are confronted by someone who says that he has risen from the dead. We might reply, in the way we have indicated, by saying that things like that do not happen. The man might reply, with Geach's approval I think,

15

that this is perfectly true. He might go on to say, however, that a new age has dawned, that all over the place the graves are yielding their dead. What are we to say in face of such testimony? It must be remembered that the bodies with which we are confronted are new bodies. But in this case, if the new bodies are *entirely* unconnected (5) with the old bodies, it is logically possible for more than one person to claim to be John Jones raised from the dead. In that case, as we have already seen, the most we could say is that these people possess remarkably similar or exactly similar traits of character and memories to John Jones, but the question of identity would not arise. (Cf p. 17. See also [29] p. 385). If, on the other hand, the new bodies are connected with the old bodies in some way or other as Geach suggested in a one–one relation, why should we say that the previous bodies had died? But, of course we know *with certainty* that all human beings die. Even if the second supposition considered above is conceivable, it does not follow that it makes sense *now* for us to say that men live after death. Similarly, even though a story can be invented about surgeons failing to find a man's heart, this does not prevent us from saying *now* that 'I have no heart' is a piece of nonsense.

We have concentrated in this chapter on questions concerning bodily life after death, the problem of identifying the risen body and the bearing this has on the notion of the existence of a disembodied spirit. But very little has been said about the *life* that is to be enjoyed beyond the grave. It has been said with good reason that the hope of life after death is often connected with the hope of seeing loved ones again, of taking up broken relationships, of righting wrongs committed long ago, and so on. All these activities depend on a continuance not merely of the individuals involved, but of the forms of life in which they participated, and the social institutions connected with these ways of living. When Jesus was asked which of the many husbands a woman had had would be hers after death, he rejected the question. He said that there was no giving and taking in marriage in heaven. Now tied up with marital relationships is a complex of other relationships: child–parent relationships, relationships between brothers and sisters, relationships between lovers, and so on. If the situations in which such relationships have their meaning cannot be spoken of except within the context of this human life here on earth, how can one speak of taking up and continuing these relationships after death? What is to be made of the hope of meeting fathers, mothers, brothers, sisters, friends, lovers, after death? Of course,

16

in one sense of 'know', I know my father if I can pick him out in an identity parade. But that is not what is normally meant by knowing someone as one's father. The knowledge we have in mind can only be understood in terms of the child–parent relationship. The question arises, then, of how one can know one's father after death without being his son, how one can know one's lover without still being a lover oneself, or how one can be a friend without the bonds of friendship. Yet no one suggests that the features of this life which make these relationships the wonderful and terrible things they can be are perpetuated beyond this life. It is of little use suggesting that what we have is a state of affairs in which all these things are remembered: where lovers remember their love, parents their children, and friends each other. The crucial question is whether they are parents, children, lovers and friends when they remember, for if they are not, then parents, lovers and friends have not been reunited, but only some strange creatures with memories of joys and sorrows no longer present.

The life which is said to exist after death is said to be beyond all change. Yet all the relationships we have mentioned depend upon change for their very meaning. Mortality is not a limitation in human relationships. On the contrary, it is a precondition of their being the kind of relationships they are. So even if all the logical difficulties about surviving death are put aside, and we entertain imaginative pictures of the world to come, these pictures themselves occasion further logical difficulties of a radical nature. (6)

What are we to say, then, in answer to the question with which we began our enquiry: Does belief in immortality rest on a mistake? Certainly, we have found that if that belief is construed as belief in the existence of a non-material body, a disembodied spirit, or a physical body, after death, it seems to be riddled with difficulties and confusions. For my part, if this were all there is to tell, I should have to conclude that belief in immortality rests, not only on one mistake, but on a large number of possible mistakes. But if this were our conclusion, should I not revise my opening remarks in which I said that a treatment of the above question would not lead us finally to anywhere of very great interest?

I said at the outset that in attempting to answer the question 'Does belief in immortality rest on a mistake?' many philosophers examined what they assumed were essential presuppositions of the belief. In the present chapter, we have noted the alleged pre-

17

suppositions and the difficulties connected with them. I have not done more than to note them. Indeed, almost every topic I have discussed in this chapter calls for more detailed treatment. Often, I have done little more than indicate lines of thought, and suggest how I might develop them. I do not pretend that my observations will satisfy philosophers who have worked on these points in detail. I decided to present nothing more than a general survey partly because of the restrictions of space imposed upon me. More importantly, I decided to do so because I believe that success or failure in resolving the logical difficulties we have noted do not have important consequences *as far as belief in immortality is concerned*. Most philosophers think that the difficulties we have considered are unsurmountable, and that therefore the presuppositions of belief in the immortality of the soul are seen to be confused. When the presuppositions of the belief collapse, the belief itself collapses.

All this, however, is based on one large assumption, namely, that the matters we have been discussing *are* necessary presuppositions of a belief in the immortality of the soul. I said that for the most part I would not question this assumption in the present chapter. It has now become necessary to state that in fact I do not think that belief in the possibility of the survival of disembodied spirits after the death of human bodies, or in the possibility of non-material bodies living on after the death of material bodies, or in the possibility of bodies resurrecting after death, are, as we have depicted them, necessary presuppositions of a belief in the immortality of the soul. Indeed, our major task is still before us, namely, to ask whether an account of a belief in the immortality of the soul can be given which is different from those we have discussed in this chapter. But we are not ready to embark on this task immediately. Before doing so, we must consider another context commonly associated with belief in the immortality of the soul, which is connected in many ways with the issues we have been considering.

The problems of whether a man lives after death, of whether the man who lives after death is the same person who died, are problems which belong in this context, not simply to problems about identity and the relation of mind and body; they are problems which are connected with certain beliefs about the *moral* relations which do or ought to hold between the life a man lives here and now, and his existence after death. Flew, for example, shows how the problem of identity is essential to a consideration of the notion of the Day of Judgement, understood as a future event:

> Now to be justly accountable, here or hereafter, for a murder, you have to be the same person as the villain who did the murder; that is a necessary, though by no means sufficient, condition of responsibility. ([6] p. 1)

Flew thinks that this condition cannot be fulfilled by anyone who dies before the Great Day. We have considered good reasons for this conclusion. The moral attitudes associated with the Day of Judgement can, to some extent, be examined independently of the problems we have been considering. What can be said is this: for many philosophers, it is important to establish the possibility of life after death at the very least, since without that possibility, crucial events, namely, corpses living again, are not going to take place. Furthermore, if such events do not take place, there are no empirical data which can serve as reasons for taking up certain attitudes to this present life, attitudes which constitute a certain kind of belief in the immortality of the soul. If our moral strivings in this world are in some sense dependent on our living again in a world to come, then, clearly, if it turns out that we do not in fact live after death, or that it makes no sense to speak of living after death, this will have serious consequences for the ways we regard our moral strivings. It seems that for many people, immortality, construed as some kind of life after death, constitutes a vindication of the beliefs and values to which they adhere in this life. Before considering the possibility of a radically different conception of immortality, we must first examine this notion of vindication.

2 Survival After Death and the Vindication of Belief

In the previous chapter we assumed that a belief in immortality entails some kind of survival after death. We examined various kinds of survival which might be involved, and found that they all involve serious logical and empirical difficulties. In many ways, we saw that the notion of bodily survival of a physical kind after death is central to the belief that the *same* person lives again after his death. On the other hand, this notion inherits as many difficulties as the notion of disembodied existence after death or the notion of non-material bodies surviving death. And, as Professor Geach admits, there is no philosophical reason to expect that at some future date the graves will yield their dead. Nevertheless, Geach says, this is the faith that Christians have:

> That faith is not going to be shaken by inquiries about bodies burned to ashes or eaten by beasts; those who might well suffer such death in martyrdom were those who were most confident of a glorious reward in the resurrection. One who shares that hope will hardly wish to take out an occultistic or philosophical insurance policy, to guarantee some sort of survival as an annuity, in case God's promise of resurrection should fail. ([9] p. 29)

It seems that there are other considerations which make a man think it rational to hope for the resurrection of the dead, and I want to consider some of these in the present chapter.

It might be said that there is an important connection between the lives we think we ought to live here and now on earth, and the life we are to live after death. That latter life is something we inherit, and what needs to be made explicit is the nature of, and the reasons for, the inheritance. An attempt might be made to make these matters explicit as follows. People think that they can do what they ought to do without any thought of God. If, in thinking this, they are making a psychological claim, they are perfectly right. A man can believe that murder and adultery are wrong without thinking that these wrongs are forbidden by God. Furthermore, it is also true to say that not all our appraisals of good and evil are logically dependent on a knowledge of God. Geach argues that knowing that lying is generally blameworthy does not depend on its being a received revelation, since any revelation which contradicted this moral truth would itself be worthless. Geach says,

> Sir Arnold Lunn has jeered at unbelievers for esteeming truth-fulness apart from any supernatural hopes or fears, and has quoted with approval a remark of Belloc that one can't be loyal to an abstraction like truth; a pagan Greek would have retorted that Lunn and Belloc were *akolastoi*, incorrigibly wicked, if they could not see directly the badness of lying. ([10] p. 120)

Therefore Geach does not want to contend that knowledge of God is a prerequisite of *any* moral knowledge. But we do need a know-ledge of God, Geach wants to say, in order to see that we may not do evil that good may come. 'Now when I speak of "not doing evil that good may come", what I mean is that certain sorts of act are such *bad things to do* that they must never be done to secure any good or avoid any evil' ([10] p. 120). Geach wants to argue that this principle actually follows from a certain conception of God.

What would be the difference between two men, both of whom agreed that something was morally wrong, but only one of whom accepts the principle Geach has in mind?

> Suppose that A and B are agreed that adultery is a bad sort of behaviour, but that A accepts the principle of not doing evil that good may come, whereas B rejects it. Then in A's moral deliberations adultery is simply out: As Aristotle said, there can be no deliberating when and how and with whom to commit it (EN 1107 a 16). For B, on the other hand, the *prima facie* objection to adultery is defeasible, and in some circumstances he may decide: Here and now adultery is the best thing. ([10] p. 121)

Again, it is psychologically possible to hold to the principle of not doing evil that good may come without any thought of God, but, according to Geach, it is not logically consistent to do so. Why is this the case?

22

When Geach spoke of the man who was prepared to contemplate adultery being a good thing in certain circumstances, and contrasted him unfavourably with the man for whom adultery was simply out, he might have given the impression that adultery was out for the latter simply because he thought adultery to be wrong for various moral reasons. But this impression would be rather misleading, since in order for 'Adultery is out' to be a rational attitude, Geach thinks it necessary that an answer be given to the question why adultery is wrong. What is important here is the way Geach thinks this question must be answered. He says that 'One obviously relevant sort of reply to a question "Why shouldn't I?" is an appeal to something the questioner wants, and cannot get if he does so-and-so. I maintain that only such a reply is relevant and rational' ([10] p. 121). Geach, in this insistence, is an example of a powerful and recurring tradition in moral philosophy. Within this tradition, morality is seen as a guide to human action. The human agent is confronted by a number of alternative actions, and morality, it is thought, will tell him which are the ones he ought to choose. This is the sort of advice Geach seems to ask of morality. If a man asks why he should refrain from committing adultery, the only reason Geach seems prepared to accept as rational is that so acting will, in the end, get a man what he wants. Morality, then, is a way of acting which secures for a man what he wants. But this seems a very strange view of morality. Does morality in fact remove the familiar obstacles which often stand between a man and the goals he aims for: lack of resources, lack of money, lack of health, etc.? Obviously, it does not. Peter Winch makes this point and then goes on to consider whether it could be said that morality helps one around moral difficulties, for example, the difficulty of extending one's business legally and without loss of reputation, where doing so involves something morally questionable:

> Morality, we are told, is a guide which helps him round his difficulty. But were it not for morality there would be no difficulty! This is a strange sort of guide, which first puts obstacles in our path and then shows us the way round them. Would it not be far simpler and more rational to be shot of the thing altogether? Then we could get on with the matter in hand, whatever it is. ([38] p. 4)

What many philosophers have done is to try to answer this question on its own terms. When a man points out that acting in a certain

23

way hinders the achievement of certain goals, and that since this way of acting is what morality demands, he is going to put it aside as an unnecessary hindrance, they have replied by saying that really, if he took greater notice, he would find that disregarding moral considerations did not enable him to achieve what he wanted at all. Things being as they are, a man gets what he wants by heeding to moral considerations. Thus, morality is seen as an obstacle, but a necessary one, given the present situation. As Geach puts the matter, 'to choose to lack a virtue would be to choose a maimed life, ill-adapted to this difficult and dangerous world' ([10] p. 122–3). Glaucon, in Plato's *Republic*, agrees that in the present situation, it is in a man's interests to pay lip-service to morality. But Glaucon, in the story of the magical Ring of Gyges, imagines the situation as being different, where a man can make himself invisible at will. Such a man, he argues, would be regarded as a fool if he did not do wrong with impunity, although people would still keep up the pretence of condemning him for his actions. Winch says that 'Glaucon's challenge has haunted moral philosophy ever since' ([38] p. 5). Philosophers have tried to show why, even in such circumstances, it would still be in a person's interests to pay heed to moral considerations. But, from the very nature of the case, what they have to show is that, given his interests, moral actions will serve those interests better than any other kind of action. In other words, they have to show that it pays to be good. An obvious difficulty facing anyone undertaking such an enterprise is that it is far too obvious in many cases that injustice has profited the person concerned. Why have people asked for so long, 'Why do the wicked prosper?' Philippa Foot's answer to this question is that 'The reason why it seems to some people so impossibly difficult to show that justice is more profitable than injustice is that they consider in isolation particular just acts' ([8] p. 104). Mrs Foot argues that it would be extremely difficult for someone to pursue a Glauconian policy of paying lip-service to morality but at the same time be on the look-out for the opportunistic profitable evil action. Her arguments amount to saying, 'You wouldn't get away with it.' But if this is a factual prediction, and Mrs Foot seems to intend it as such, then its opposite is conceivable. What if someone did get away with it? In a criticism of Mrs Foot's arguments I imagined such a person on his death-bed. I imagined a person, surely not hard to find, who refused to take Mrs Foot's advice at the outset of life about the probability of profit being on the side of justice. I said that certainly, at that early time, he had good reason to choose justice rather than injustice, but, being a gambler by nature, he chose injustice. As it happened, things went well for him. He profited in every way he wished to profit. Now, on his death-bed, he looks back over his life with relish, 'It was certainly a lucky day for me when I gambled against the odds on lying, cheating, swindling and betraying paying off.' We want to say that what this man did was wrong. The fact that in facing death he shows no remorse is but an additional mark against him. But Mrs Foot can give no account of this judgement. She must admit that he has in fact lived the best kind of life he could have lived. Her only consolation is that such a man, like everyone else, had good reason to choose justice rather than injustice. But he chose injustice! ([17] pp. 59–60) I also considered, in criticising Mrs Foot, the case of the man whose just policies brought him face to face with death. I contended that her analysis can give no account of the man who dies for the sake of justice. It can only give an account of the man who dies as the result of justice. Since the only reason for the general survey of probabilities was to show a man what is in his interest, when facing death, the person involved has a superior measure with which to assess the profitableness of just actions. I said that death cannot appear in Mrs Foot's list of profits, since that in terms of which the profit is to be assessed no longer exists. Therefore, the prospect of certain death always makes it unprofitable to play the game that justice demands ([17] pp. 50–1). (1)

Now it would appear that Geach has an answer to both criticisms. First, Geach would not agree that we must say that the gambler on his death-bed surveying with relish his life of injustice has lived the best life he could have lived. This is because we falsely assumed that what is in his interest can be assessed simply in terms of the course his life has taken. If we believe in God, the story does not end there. On the contrary, if God is a voluntary agent, Geach argues, he will direct men to his own ends in a rational fashion. Thus, the laws he has promulgated are laws which constitute what men really need. Men who know that lying is generally wrong have had the divine law promulgated to them, even if they do not recognise it as such. Without God, it is always possible to cite instances where a man's policy of just actions has led him to disaster. But once the pursuit of justice has been seen as obedience to the will of God, it can no longer be thought that such a pursuit may not be in a man's best interests. Geach says:

25

We cannot balance against our obedience to God some good to be gained, or evil to be avoided, by disobedience. For such good or evil could in fact come to us only in the order of God's Providence; we cannot secure good or avoid evil, either for ourselves or for others, in God's despite and by disobedience. And neither reason nor revelation warrants the idea that God is at all likely to be lenient with those who presumptuously disobey his law because of the way they have worked out the respective consequence of obedience and disobedience. ([10] p. 129)

In the same way, Geach can say that the man who faces death as a result of his policy of justice is wrong to envy those who act unjustly and seem to enjoy life nevertheless. Again, the trouble with such a man is that his calculation is based on too narrow a perspective. It is true, Geach says, that

The wicked can for the moment use God's creation in defiance of God's commandments. But this is a sort of miracle or mystery; as St. Paul said, God has made the creature subject to vanity against its will. It is reasonable to expect, if the world's whole *raison d'être* is to effect God's good pleasure, that the very natural agents and operations of the world should be such as to frustrate and enrage and torment those who set their wills against God's. If things are not at present like this, that is only a gratuitous mercy, on whose continuance the sinner has no reason to count. 'The world shall fight with him against the unwise . . . . Yea, a mighty wind shall stand up against them, and like a storm shall blow them away.' ([10] p. 129)

It was possible on Mrs Foot's account to imagine a situation where it did not pay to be good, and to ask why one should be good nevertheless. No moral reasons could be given, since, clearly, that would beg the question under consideration. Yet, we should not want to say that men are fools when they still pursue the good in these situations. But Geach's arguments do not allow us to drive a wedge between justice and what is in a man's interests. If we extend our perspective, Geach argues, beyond our limited human perspective, to consider human actions as God sees them, we shall have reason to believe that it always pays to be good. The fulfilment of God's will is at the same time the fulfilment of man's will. Men are not fools when they refuse to be influenced by the cal-

26

culation of the consequences of pursuing justice in this life. Such calculation may lead to unfavourable consequences predominating over favourable consequences. But such arithmetic is necessarily spurious. The final calculation is in the hands of God, and the outcome is always on the side of justice, even if that outcome is beyond the grave. Thus, we can see the way in which belief in immortality is thought to serve as a rational foundation or a rational end for the pursuit of goodness. In this world, there may be moments when one wonders whether justice and goodness are worth pursuing. One's immediate reading of the scale of probabilities makes the matter look doubtful. At such times, Geach would say, what we need to do is to extend the scale so that it includes an assessment of life after death. Once we do this we find that we have good reason to suppose that moral beliefs are always vindicated in the end. Thus, even in the darkest hour in this life, the believer can say that all things work together for good to them that love God.

To what extent does Geach's argument achieve what it set out to do, namely, to show why moral considerations should move the will, why they should make a person choose one course of action rather than another? If one thinks that it is essential for a moral philosopher to meet Glaucon's challenge on its own terms, or agrees with Mrs Foot that those who accept Thrasymachus's premiss – that injustice is more profitable than justice – and yet want to deny his conclusion – that a man who has the strength to get away with injustice has a reason to follow this as the best way of life – are in a dubious position, then one will think that Geach's case is the best that can be made. What better incentive to justice and disincentive to injustice than to show that in fact it is always the case that adherence to justice pays and that it is never the case that anyone's strength is sufficient to change this state of affairs?

Yet all this ignores the fundamental question which has to be answered: *Should* the moral philosopher accept Glaucon's challenge on its own terms? In doing so, might he not be falsifying the character of the considerations he is examining, namely, moral considerations? True, Geach's arguments offer incentives and disincentives to the man who is considering whether he ought to heed moral considerations or not, but have these incentives and disincentives anything to do with morality? I suggest not. Sometimes there is an ambiguity in Geach's discussion which obscures these matters. But once the ambiguity is revealed, where he stands is quite clear. Geach, praising Mrs Foot, says that according to her,

> Moral virtues . . . are habits of action and avoidance; and they are such as a man cannot rationally choose to go without, any more than he can rationally choose to be blind, paralytic, or stupid; to choose to lack a virtue would be to choose a maimed life, ill-adapted to this difficult and dangerous world. But if you opt for virtue, you opt for being the sort of man who *needs* to act virtuously (just as if you choose to take up smoking you opt to be the kind of man who *needs* to smoke). ([10] pp. 122–3)

The comparison between virtue and smoking is limited, to say the least, and to speak of *opting* for virtue is extremely queer, but putting these matters aside for the moment, let us explore what Geach actually says about the two cases. He says that the man who chooses to smoke chooses to be the kind of man who needs to smoke, but is this true? Men may choose to smoke for various reasons: in order to conform to the habits of the circle of friends they belong to, because they believe it is a sign of maturity, because they want to impress their girl-friends who like to see men smoke, or because they like smoking. In all the cases except the last, the reason for smoking is outside the activity of smoking itself. It would be natural to say of a man who smoked for these reasons that he only needs to smoke because of these other considerations, which is the same as saying that it is not the smoking itself that the man needs. In the last case, however, it is the smoking itself that the man has come to need, and in order to communicate the need to others, he would have to talk about the delight of smoking. If someone did not understand that delight, he could not make his need intelligible to him. As I have said, the analogy between virtue and smoking is extremely limited, if present at all (think of what it makes sense to say if someone says that he has decided to give either one up), but forgetting that fact for present purposes, one can see that the same ambiguity is to be found in Geach's discussion of virtue. Instead of speaking of *opting* for virtue, since this already falsifies the issue, let us think of the man who has a regard for generosity, kindness, justice, and so on. What has won his regard? It might be the case that for a given individual this question can be answered in terms of the success, prestige, reputation, etc., which paying lip-service to such things brings in the community. If this were not the case, he would soon give up bothering about such things. But in the case of another person, his regard, it seems, cannot be explained in this way. When asked why he thinks he ought to be kind, generous and just, he answers, not in terms of what so acting brings, but in terms of what kindness, generosity and justice are. Trading on the ambiguity in his use of 'needs' – 'if you opt for virtue, you opt for being the sort of man who *needs* to act virtuously' – Geach may mean that it is love of virtue that creates the need for virtue in a man, or he may mean that it can be shown to him, independently of what virtue means, that he needs it. Unfortunately, this latter alternative is what Geach seems to have in mind. Virtue is what gets one what one wants in this dangerous world. Here, the assessment of what one wants is clearly meant to be independent of the proposed means of getting it. But when we are confronted with two men, one of whom loves justice, kindness and generosity, without thought for what they bring, while the other thinks only of what they bring, do we not want to say different things about them? Do we not want to say that only one of them loves justice, while the other's love is a mere pretence, a façade? That this is so is shown by the fact that when the situation changes, when it no longer pays to be good, the man who pursued the virtues only for external reasons soon gives up his love of virtue. But, notice, even if the change in the situation never comes about, even if it always remains the case that it pays to be good, the difference between the two men remains unaltered, for what determines that difference is the relation within which they stand to the pursuit of virtue. A woman may never find out that a man loved her only for her money, but the fact that her money does not run out does not change the character of his love. Geach argues that we can rest assured that it always pays to be good; God's providence ensures that in the final analysis this is always the case. No matter, for even if for an infinite duration success follows fast on the heels of virtue, there will be an eternal distinction between the man who was moved to pity, and the man who 'pitied' because he was moved by love of success. So asking 'Does it pay to be good?' is already to falsify the character of moral considerations. As Winch says,

. . . the form of the question suggests that we must look *outside* morality for something on which morality can be based. But the moment we do this, then 'what is commended is not morality itself', for surely if the commendation is in terms of some further advantage, the connection between that advantage and morality can only be a contingent one. ([38] p. 7)

At first, Geach seems, as I have said, to answer Winch's point by trying to get rid of the contingent connection between morality and advantage, but he misunderstands the contingency involved. Geach argues as if the reason why there is a problem about showing why it pays to be good is because these advantages *may not come about*. He argues that there is a necessary connection between morality and advantage because God will always see to it that the advantages *always* come about. But that is not the kind of contingency I take Winch to be referring to. On the contrary, the reason why he says rightly that there must be a contingent connection between morality and advantage is because it is always possible to distinguish between a concern for moral considerations and a concern for advantage; that the former is independent of, and qualitatively different from, the latter. That is why Winch says, 'And it does not matter how strong a contingent connection it is; it will still not be 'morality itself' which is being commended' ([38] pp. 7–8).

It has been seen that construing belief in the immortality of the soul as the final state which gives men good reasons for acting in certain ways now falsifies the character of moral regard. It certainly allows no room for anything that might be meant by the spirituality of the soul. It seems to me that if people lead a certain kind of life simply because of the final set of consequences to which it leads, they are indifferent to that way of life. But, it might be argued, this is clearly wrong. In the example we are considering, people are not indifferent to practising virtues, since only if they practise them will they attain immortality, understood here as life after death. If they had not practised virtue they would not have fulfilled these ends. But here, the end, what they wish to achieve, is all-important, the means, the godly life, relatively unimportant. This kind of life *happens* to be the one that leads to this result. But what if another kind of life, the antithesis of the one one has lived, happened to be the one which led to survival after death, would one then lead that life? If the end is all-important, why not? And even if the end is always secured by living an admirable life, there is still a distinction between a regard for what is admirable and a regard for the end in question. Geach's argument has a deceptive character, since until one examines it closely, it seems as if he is giving an account of the absolute nature of moral claims on one's

30

life. He says that if 'you opt for chastity, then you opt to become the sort of person who *needs* to be chaste; and then for you, as Aristotle said, there can be no deliberating when and with whom to commit adultery; adultery is out' ([10] p. 123). But we have to remember that on Geach's view, adultery is out because in God's providence adultery is one of the kind of actions which it does not pay to perform. One may think that one can get away with adultery, but one cannot. But why should any of the facts mentioned hitherto cast any light on moral considerations? The only difference between a man who chooses not to commit adultery because he thinks that it might not pay to do so, and the man who does not commit adultery because he knows it does not pay to do so is the difference between two gamblers, both of whom back the right horse, but only one of whom knows with certainty that it is going to win. But they are both worlds removed from the man who would not commit adultery whether it paid to do so or not. For the latter, committing adultery is not an alternative to be considered, since it is his regard for fidelity which determines what the alternatives open to him are to be. For him, 'It is adultery' is a means, not an object, of assessment. On Geach's terms, adultery is out as an alternative because it does not pay, it is not in the person's interests to commit it. What I am insisting on is that it is love of fidelity which determines what is out, not what is out which determines the worthwhileness of fidelity. Morality is not dependent on the odds regarding what is and what is not advantageous, no matter how certain those odds are said to be.

Why does Geach want to show that it pays to be good? The answer is that he thinks that unless he does this, he must follow post-Kantian moral philosophers in saying that what one means by good actions are those which are done from a sense of duty. He sees, quite rightly, that terrible actions can be done from this motive. But in terms of the thesis being proposed, as long as a man is acting from a sense of duty he is acting from the highest motives: 'If a young Nazi machine-guns a column of refugees till he bleeds to death, instead of retiring for medical treatment, is not his Sense of Duty something to fill us with awe?' ([10] p. 122). Geach concludes, 'To myself, it seems clear that although '*You mustn't*' said in this peculiar way may psychologically work as a final answer to 'Why shouldn't I?', it is no rational answer at all' ([10] p. 122). In searching for a rational answer, Geach turns to the attempt to show why it is in a man's interests to be good. But it is this that constitutes his fatal mistake. When he rejected the sense of duty as a guide to what men ought to do, he sought another guide, namely, what is in man's interests. What needs to be done is to give up the conception of morality as a guide to conduct, and to see that the beliefs and ideals for which one has a regard are themselves the terms in which we see what we ought to do, the alternatives which face us and the consequences of our actions. As Winch points out ([38] p. 10), this means that men will sometimes agree on the description of a situation but disagree about what is to be done, but also may sometimes even fail to agree on how the situation is to be described. Some men will see a problem where others see none. What, then, are our conculsions on these matters? They have been expressed well by Winch as follows:

> I think the situation is something like this. If one looks at a certain style of life and asks what there is in it which makes it worth while, one will find nothing there. One may indeed describe it in terms which bring out 'what one sees in it', but the use of these terms already presupposes that one does see it from a perspective from which it matters. The words will fall flat on the ears of someone who does not occupy such a perspective even though he is struggling to attain it. If one tries to find in the object of contemplation that which makes it admirable, what one will in fact see is the admiration and applause which surrounds it. ([38] p. 24)

Earlier, Winch discusses the Glauconian question that Tolstoy makes Marie, the retarded young girl, ask Father Sergius when she seduces him. It is the question which Geach thinks it all-important to answer. Here is the relevant scene from Tolstoy's story:

> 'What is your name?' he asked, trembling all over and feeling that he was overcome and that his desire had already passed beyond control. 'Marie. Why?' She took his hand and kissed it, and then put her arm around his waist and pressed him to herself. 'What are you doing?' he said. 'Marie, you are a devil!' 'Oh, perhaps. What does it matter?' And embracing him she sat down with him on the bed. ([30] p. 343)

Earlier, as Winch says, Sergius had overcome his lust by chopping off one of his fingers. Then, lust had been seen as a

32

temptation to be met and overcome within the context of religious belief:

> That is to say [Winch says] it was not then a case of setting the satisfaction of his desire alongside the demands of his religion and choosing between them. The fulfilment of his religious duties was not then for him an object to be achieved. But this is what it had become for him at the time he succumbed to temptation and this indeed is precisely why he succumbed. Marie's question 'What does it matter?' invited a judgment explaining why religious purity is more important than the satisfaction of lust, a comparison, as it were, between two different objects. And no such judgment was possible. I do not mean that earlier, at the time of his strength, Sergius *could* have answered the question; the point is that, from that earlier perspective, the question did not arise for him. ([38] p. 22)

It does not matter how impressive the attempts to meet the Glauconian challenge, how splendid the prospects displayed before us tend to be, 'there is still always another question to be asked', as J. L. Stocks said, 'not a question whether in achieving this you will not perhaps diminish your chances of achieving something still more important; but a question of another kind. "There is a decency required", as Browning said; and this demand of decency is prepared to sacrifice, in the given case, any purpose whatever' ([28] p. 77). Geach tries to meet Glaucon's challenge by appealing to what he takes to be God's purposes, immortal life governed by divine providence. The consequences of pursuing virtue in this life may be disastrous, but they cannot be disastrous in the long run. But this kind of argument simply will not do. It is not a matter of adding more and more impressive consequences. In doing so, Geach is like the man Kierkegaard described, who 'at the outset . . . took the wrong way and then continued to go on further and further along this false way' ([13] p. 48). What is needed is the recognition that moral considerations cannot be accounted for purely in terms of purposive action. They constitute an additional principle of discrimination; they have to do with the *character* which action may or may not have.

Furthermore, when an attempt is made, such as Geach's, to demonstrate how moral endeavour is based on a certain conception of divine providence, so far from the case being made, the antithesis and tension between moral considerations and a prudential providence are made explicit. For Geach, in the end,

33

the question why I should pursue virtue is answered by an enumeration of the consequences of disobeying God's commands. But what if someone asks why he should obey God's commands? Geach replies:

> This is really an insane question. For Prometheus to defy Zeus made sense because Zeus had not made Prometheus and had only limited power over him. A defiance of an Almighty God is insane: it is like trying to cheat a man to whom your whole business is mortgaged and who you know is well aware of your attempts to cheat him. ([10] p. 126)

But this analogy is completely misplaced. The businessman and the man who tries to cheat him are in fact playing the same game: they would both be concerned with the same end, namely, whether certain goods are going to be paid for or not, or whether certain monies are going to get into the wrong hands or not. In other words, both the businessman and his would-be cheater share the same criteria of success and failure. Both would recognise and have to admit it if the other won. But this is not so in the clash between moral and prudential considerations. Here, 'success' and 'failure' do not mean the same within each category. Hence, since moral defiance would *not* mean defiance in the hope that what is said to be prudential turns out not to be prudential after all, such defiance makes sense even in face of a prudential providence which is certain because it is said to be ordained by God. Of course, Geach is right in saying that a man who defied a god so conceived would be irrational if he wanted to prosper (in a prudential sense) in the end. Given this context, no one can defeat God at his own game. Nevertheless, it is still open to someone to say what he thinks of such a game, since saying that you think a certain game is a rotten kind of game is quite compatible with losing at it. This has been brought out well by Rush Rhees in the following remarks:

> Suppose you had to explain to someone who had no idea at all of religion or of what a belief in God was. Could you do it in this way? – By proving to him that there must be a first cause – a Something – and that this Something is more powerful (whatever this means) than anything else: so that you would not have been conceived or born at all but for the operation of Something, and Something might wipe out the existence of everything

at any time? Would this give him any sense of the wonder and the glory of God? Would he not be justified if he answered, 'What a horrible idea! Like a Frankenstein without limits, so that you cannot escape it. The most ghastly nightmare! ... If my first and chief reason for worshipping God had to be a belief that a super-Frankenstein would blast me to hell if I did not, then I hope I should have the decency to tell this being, who is named Almighty God, to go ahead and blast'. ([25] pp. 112–13)

Why does Geach think that such a response to the unlimited power would be irrational? Is it not because he assumes that since a regard for decency must pay in the end, what pays in the end must be regarded as decent? Belief in decency or belief in God must be vindicated in the end. Recognition of the payment must, given a man has his wits about him and is not stubborn or foolish, lead to submission to the will of God. Geach says that 'Nebuchad-nezzar had it forced on his attention that only by God's favour did his wits hold together from one end of a blasphemous sentence to another – and so he saw that there was nothing for him but to bless and glorify the King of Heaven, who is able to abase those who walk in pride' ([10] pp. 126–7). But what sort of a change is Geach depicting here? Surely, it is nothing more than the change in a man who comes to realise that he has backed the wrong horse. It is not a change of character at all. One can imagine a man who comes to see that he was wrong in promoting a certain business venture since the profit he had envisaged at the time did not come his way. So he promotes another business venture. This change simply constitutes a change in what he promotes; it does not constitute a change of character. Geach depicts the believer's reasons for believing in God in the same way – as a balancing of prudential policies. 'We cannot balance against our obedience to God some good to be gained, or evil to be avoided, by dis-obedience. For such good or evil could in fact come to us only in the order of God's Providence' ([10] p. 129). Geach's case is stronger than I described it a moment ago, but its character is no different. Geach is not saying: balance the profits of disobeying God and the profits of obeying God, and you will find *more* profits on the side of obeying God. He is saying something more than that, namely, that the profits of obeying God are the only profits there are, and hence that there is not even any question of balancing anything against them. But this quantitative change in

35

the amount of profit envisaged does not change the character of the argument or the character of the advice one can give to an unbeliever on the basis of it, advice which Rush Rhees describes as follows:

> Is the reason for not worshipping the devil instead of God that God is stronger than the devil? God will get you in the end, the devil will not be able to save you from his fury, and then you will be *for* it. 'Think of your future, boy, and don't throw away your chances.' What a creeping and vile sort of thing religion must be. ([25] p. 113)

Geach thinks that because the divine power he is depicting is unlimited, the recognition of this fact is in some way rescued from the charge of servility.

> I shall be told . . . that since I am saying not: It is your supreme moral duty to obey God, but simply: It is insane to set about defying an Almighty God, my attitude is plain power-worship. So it is: but it is worship of the Supreme Power, and as such is wholly different from, and does not carry with it, a cringing attitude towards earthly powers. An earthly potentate does not compete with God, even unsuccessfully: he may threaten all manner of afflictions, but only from God's hands can any affliction actually come upon us. If we fully realize this, we shall have such fear of God as destroys all earthly fear: 'I will show you whom you shall fear', said Jesus Christ to his disciples. ([10] p. 127)

Geach may be right in thinking that he has removed all cringing attitudes to earthly powers, but he has replaced them with a picture of a cringing attitude to a heavenly power. True, the slave has changed his master, or rather, has recognised who has been his master all along, but he is still the slave, and he still cringes. The picture is no different when Geach says, 'The fear of God of which I have spoken is such fear as restrains even the wish to disobey him; not merely servile fear, which restrains the outward act, but leaves behind the wish "If only I could do it and get away with it!" ' ([10] p. 128). Nothing Geach has said bears this out, but even if this were not the case, it would hardly be sufficient. The above description of the fear of God would be quite consistent with that of a person so beaten and subjected by a tyrant that all

36

thought of resistance had been killed in him, all that remained being the fear of disobedience. Would anyone accept this as an adequate picture of the fear of God which is said to be the beginning of wisdom? It will not do either to say that a man may begin by fearing God in this way and then later grow to love him, since if that love is to be depicted rightly, it would involve giving it even if all the reasons for fearing God which Geach has enumerated were absent. Clearly, this is not what Geach has in mind, since although he says that his arguments do not bring one to see how it is possible for a believer to love God and call him Father, this not being a product of our natural knowledge of God, he agrees with Hobbes 'that gratitude for God's benefits would not be a sufficient ground for *unreserved* obedience if it were severed from fear of God's irresistible power' ([10] p. 129).

For Geach, there seems to be only one conception of power, victory, triumph, etc., where God and the powers of the world are concerned. It is a power, victory and triumph which the powers of the world think they possess, but which are really possessed by God. Thus, when it is said that 'all things work together for good to them that love God', it appears that for Geach, the goodness involved is one that all men would recognise if they were not unreasonable, stubborn or foolish. If you do not believe in God, your belief will not be vindicated, but if it is God you believe in, vindication in the end is certain. God and the powers of the world seem to be playing the same game, but only God ever wins. The good towards which loving God aims is, apparently, one which all men want, and one which can be used to measure belief in God against other conflicting beliefs. But what is the common measure Geach has in mind? Does not searching for such a common measure obscure the fact that there is a tension, a radical opposition, between the ways of God and the ways of the world? There are occasions when there is a clash between what the world calls disaster and what the believers call disaster. This is not because the worldy-minded are miscalculating, while the godly are calculating properly. On the contrary, the point is that different things are called disastrous because different conceptions of disaster are involved. The same would be true of any comparison between God's power and the forces of darkness:

The power of God is a *different* power from the power of the devil. But if you said that God is *more* powerful than the devil –

then I should not understand you, because I should not know what sort of measure you used. ([25] p. 113)

There is no concept of vindication which is shared by 'prudence', 'morality', 'God's power' and 'the power of the Devil'. Geach is searching for a notion of ultimate vindication which all men can recognise, but the search is a futile one. It is true that many may turn to God searching for victories and compensations which are extensions of worldly victories and compensations. When it is suggested to them that such an outcome is not to come about they reply by asking what, in that case, is the point of bothering to obey God's commands? Given their motives, there is no point. It is only when a man has become absorbed by the love of God that he ceases to ask such questions, not because he is sure of his profit, but because profit has nothing to do with the character of his love. The immortality of his soul has to do, not with its existence after death and all the consequences that is supposed to carry with it, but with his participation in God's life, in his contemplation of divine love. That being so, it is not the case that immortality is assessed by some conception of goodness which is a common measure between it and the ways of the world. On the contrary, it is the conception of immortality which determines what is to be called good by those who strive for it. Vindication, victory, triumph, etc. are now understood *in terms of* immortality; they are not the things in terms of which it is measured. To seek an external justification for why a man should be concerned about his immortal soul is to destroy the character of that concern. To try to show that one should worship God because he will win in the end, is not to talk of worshipping God at all. As Rush Rhees says, '. . . any natural theology which rested on a quantitative comparison between the powers of God and the power of physical agents or operations – or: a quantitative comparison between the physical effects of God's power and the physical effects of anything else – would be a pretty unholy sort of thing' ([25] p. 113). Rhees reminds us that 'When Satan said that dominion over this world had been left to him, Jesus did not contradict him' ([25] p. 113). What we have to remember is that according to Christian teaching, when light came into this world, the darkness did not comprehend it. If the immortality of the soul has something to do with this conception of light, it will never be understood by seeking to discover common measures, however impressive, which it might share with the darkness. When it is said that such common

38

measures have been found, and that in terms of them the vindication of the light over the darkness can be demonstrated, it is almost certain that what one is in fact talking about is the vindication of the darkness in disguise. In this chapter, I have been attempting to show how easily this can happen in the case of the immortality of the soul.

3 Eternal Life and the Immortality of the Soul

As far as any attempt to give an account of the notion of immortality is concerned, the last two chapters have been negative in character. In the first, we considered difficulties involved in construing the immortality of the soul as some kind of existence after death, whether that existence be thought of as the existence of a physical body, a non-material body or a disembodied existence. In the second, we considered difficulties in certain views of the immortality of the soul connected with notions of divine providence. Such views sought to provide a rational basis for moral considerations, a reason why we should be good, but succeeded only in depicting concerns which seemed antithetical to moral considerations. At this point, many would say that it would be appropriate to admit that the notion of the immortality of the soul is the product of a number of mistakes: mistakes about the grammar of concepts such as 'self', 'I', 'existence', 'death', 'personal identity', etc., and mistakes about the characteristic roles of moral considerations. But these conclusions are mistaken. They are based on the assumption that what we have taken to be presuppositions of belief in the immortality of the soul really are necessary presuppositions of the belief. But what if this were not the case? What if belief in the immortality of the soul, so far from being the product of prudence, had close connections with certain moral beliefs? What if belief in the immortality of the soul does not entail belief in survival after death? Would not our previous conclusions have to be revised drastically? I want to try to show in the present chapter that such a revision is called for.

Other contemporary philosophers of religion have felt that in some way all the objections we have noted miss the essence of belief in the immortality of the soul. D. M. MacKinnon feels that after all the objections have had their say, there is still something left, something which the objections have not touched. He says that in order to see what people mean when they speak of death and of overcoming death, one must be prepared 'to track the language to its human source, to plot the experience of which it is

41

the expression. The experience, indeed, *which takes shape through such expression*' ([14] p. 265). Again, Stewart R. Sutherland, who does not think the objections we have considered to be as logically compelling as I tend to see them, nevertheless feels that even if such objections could be answered in their own terms, this would not bring us to the heart of the problem. This is because the terms in question are too narrow to appreciate all that is involved in belief in the immortality of the soul. Sutherland says:

> The philosopher of religion who centres his discussion of immortality and resurrection upon a literalising of the idioms of 'life after death', of 'this world and the next', must ask himself whether or not he is trying to state what should be otherwise communicated. ([29] p. 388)

Sutherland also asks whether, even if temporal continuity beyond the grave could be given sense or was a fact, it would correspond to the Christian belief in eternal life:

> But again, it must be asked, what has this to do with the Christian belief, with its language of *eternal life*? The distinction is comparable to that which Descartes drew between that which is infinite, and that which is indefinite. Eternal life is not to be equated with endless life. ([29] p. 388)

Sutherland says that attempting to show how an account could be given of a belief in immortality which does not fall foul of the objections we have been considering is the 'sort of question to which the philospher of religion should be turning his attention' ([29] p. 389). But other philosophers, Professors Flew and Geach, for example, react in very different ways. They would argue that the objections we considered in the first chapter are relevant to a belief in the immortality of the soul. The only difference between them is that Geach thinks that some of these difficulties can be overcome, while Flew would say that they cannot be overcome. Flew is in no doubt that doctrines of immortality and personal survival after death must be equated. He says that 'this alone is what gives them their huge human interest' ([4] p. 269). Similarly, Geach says that 'the question of immortality cannot even arise unless men do survive bodily death' ([9] p. 17). We must enquire whether these things are true, whether it is true that there could be no huge human interest in immortality, or that the question of immortality could not even arise, unless it implied bodily survival after death.

We have heard it said that talk about the soul demands a dualistic view of human beings; it demands that human beings be regarded as a synthesis of two distinct elements, soul and body. But is this true? Might it not be the case that those who have insisted on this assumption are, ironically, not altogether free from the dualistic views which they attack in their opponents? Flew, for example, is at pains to stress again and again that 'soul' is not a synonym for 'person' any more than 'body' is (see [7] and [6]). He wants to insist that we meet people, not the fleshy houses within which they are supposed to live, nor the mysterious incorporeal substances they are supposed to be. In so far as he is protesting against a dualistic view of human nature, his insistence is perfectly right. But, of course, it is simply not true to say that it is never the case that 'body' and 'soul' can be used in place of the word 'person'. Flew himself recognised that we sometimes use the word 'body' as a degrading reference to a person (see [7] p. 250). Nevertheless, when such a degrading reference is made, reference *is* made to the person. When a man says 'I only wanted her for her body', he does not mean that he wanted her corpse. Flew does not consider contexts where 'soul' might be used to refer to persons. Yet they are common enough. Some of these are very close to the use of 'person', but are not our immediate concern. Consider: 'He was a good soul' and 'I'm sorry for the poor old soul'. Other usages, again perfectly common, are closer to what we must investigate. To say of someone 'He'd sell his soul for money' is a perfectly natural remark. It in no way entails any philosophical theory about a duality in human nature. The remark is a moral observation about a person, one which expresses the degraded state that person is in. A man's soul, in this context, refers to his integrity, to the complex set of practices and beliefs which acting with integrity would cover for that person. Might not talk about the immortality of the soul play a similar role? If this were the case, it would not be hard to see why so many of the objections we have considered are beside the point.

At this stage, a familiar objection is likely to be made. Someone might protest that all these references to the soul beg the fundamental issue. Before one can talk about the state of a man's soul, it will be said, one must first establish that he has a soul to be in such a state. Once we establish whether there are such things as souls, we can then proceed to discuss what can be said about them, whether they can be lost, saved, survive after death, etc. etc. These objections, however, are based on a radical confusion.

43

'Every man has a soul' has been construed as if it were akin to 'Every man has a heart'. Once this has been done, the endless qualifications begin: it is a substance, but an incorporeal one, and so on. The questions also begin: Show me the soul – can its position be located? When such questions are not answered satisfactorily, the questioner, with an air of triumph, dismisses talk about the soul as an illusion. He may even congratulate himself in doing so that he has not fallen prey to a dualistic view of human nature. Yet his rejection of the notion of the soul was precisely on the grounds that if talk about the soul was to mean anything, the soul would have to be one element in a duality which constituted a human being. In this way, the very dualism he was combating influenced his own rejection of the notion of the soul. Once 'man has a soul' is thought to be akin to 'Man has a heart', it will become impossible to appreciate the way in which talk about the soul enters human discourse.

If we ask ourselves when we would consider whether a man has a soul or not, we see that this has nothing to do with any kind of empirical question. It is not like asking whether he has a larynx or not. Neither is asking whether a man would sell his soul like asking whether he would sell his body, say, for medical research. One can investigate whether a man has a larynx or not quite independently of any knowledge of the kind of life he is living. The investigation is into the existence or state of a physical object. But an investigation as to whether a man has a soul or not, or into the state his soul is in, has nothing to do with the location or examination of an object. Questions about the state of a man's soul are questions about the kind of life he is living. If the soul were some quite distinct entity within a man, it would follow that whatever a man did would not affect it. But this is not how we speak of the soul. The relation between the soul and how a man lives is not a contingent one. It is when a man sinks to depths of bestiality that someone might say that he had lost his soul. It is a man's relation to what is morally praiseworthy and fine that would determine whether this judgement was applicable or not. Similarly, it is when a man sees the degradation into which following certain materially profitable policies would bring him that he might ask, 'What profiteth it a man if he gain the whole world, and lose his own soul?' Talk about the soul, then, is not talk about some strange sort of 'thing'. On the contrary, it is a kind of talk bound up with certain moral or religious reflections a man may make on the life he is leading. Once this is recognised, once one ceases to think of the soul as a thing, as some kind of incorporeal substance, one can be brought to see that in certain contexts talk about the soul *is* a way of talking about human beings. Once this is recognised, one can no longer say, with Flew, that 'the news of the immortality of my soul would be of no more concern to me than the news that my appendix would be preserved eternally in a bottle' ([4] p. 270), since now talk about the *immortality* of the soul too would have its place within the same contexts that talk about the soul is appropriate.

I have been suggesting that terms like 'the destiny of the soul', 'losing one's soul', 'selling one's soul', 'damning one's soul', etc. are all to be understood in terms of the kind of life a person is living. To ask a question about the state of one's soul is to ask a question about the state of one's life. But how is the state of the soul to be assessed? For the believer, the state of his soul has to do with its possession or lack of spirituality, this spirituality being assessed in terms of the person's relationship to God. It is important to remember that the word 'God' is learnt in connection with worship. As Rush Rhees says, we do not learn the meaning of 'God' 'by having someone point and say "*That's* God"' ([26] p. 128). We learn what it means in coming to know how to worship, what to say to God, what to ask of him, and so on. It is in these connections that it makes sense to speak of coming to know God. Rhees makes the point as follows:

> Winston Churchill may be Prime Minister and also a company director, but I might come to know him without knowing this. But I could not know God without knowing that he was the Creator and Father of all things. That would be like saying that I might come to know Churchill without knowing that he had face, hands, body, voice or any of the attributes of a human being. ([26] p. 131)

The state of a believer's soul is seen by him in the light of its relation to beliefs in the Fatherhood and Love of God. The notions of the fatherhood and love of God constitute eternal life, the life of God, towards which the soul aspires.

Once we take note of such contexts as these, we shall give up concentrating on attempts to determine what kind of a 'thing' a soul is. The contexts I have in mind are drawn in the main from Christianity, but they are not unknown in philosophy. For example, they are expounded in Plato's 'Phaedo'. It seems to me

45

that what Plato says in this dialogue has not been accorded the merit it deserves of late. It has become fashionable to assume that Plato's remarks can be taken as a straightforward example of a dualistic view of human nature. Geach thinks, for example, that

It may be briefly stated thus: Each man's make-up includes a wholly immaterial thing, his mind and soul. It is the mind that sees and hears and feels and thinks and chooses – in a word, is conscious. The mind is the person; the body is extrinsic to the person, like a suit of clothes. Though body and mind affect one another, the mind's existence is quite independent of the body's; and there is thus no reason why the mind should not go on being conscious indefinitely after the death of the body, and even if it never again has with any body that sort of connexion which it now has. ([9] pp. 18–19)

A. G. N. Flew chides Gilbert Ryle for calling the dualistic view of human nature Cartesian, since he too wants to find it unequivocally present in Plato's 'Phaedo' ([7] p. 245). Let me make it clear that I am not denying that there is evidence in the 'Phaedo' for these remarks. The dialogue is an uneven one, and in many places Plato does speak as though by the soul he referred to a separate and independent element. This is particularly true when Plato speaks of the transmigration of souls. My quarrel with Geach and Flew is not because of what they say they find in the 'Phaedo', but because *that is all they find there*. It is amazing, for example, that Plato's discussion of the immortality of the soul can be examined without mentioning the importance he gave to the notion of purification in this connexion. If one asked Plato what this purification amounted to he would say that it had to do with turning away from the temporal to the eternal.

The man who is a prey to the temporal, for Plato, is the man who is at the mercy of his desires and passions, desires and passions which determine his activities, but which he does not understand. He is depicted as practising popular rather than philosophical virtue. He barters pleasure for pleasure and pain for pain. This is true, even when he seems to be doing morally commendable deeds, since the deeds are never pure, they are not the product of moral spontaneity. For example, a man may die an apparently courageous death, but in fact dies simply because he fears public scorn more. Now, how does Plato characterise such

46

an act? There is thought involved, a weighing of consequences, etc. This being so, one would expect to find him talking of such an act as the product of a man's soul. But without a doubt, Plato sees all instances of popular virtue as belonging to the body. In these contexts, clearly, one cannot understand Plato's distinction between soul and body in terms of a Cartesian dualism. His distinction is much closer to that which Christians have had in mind when they have distinguished between that which is of this world and that which is not of this world, between worldliness and other-worldliness. Plato speaks of the man who is at the mercy of his desires as one who lacks order in his soul. Order is given through bringing to bear an unchanging demand on the flux of desires. This demand is the demand of decency. It brings a moral scrutiny to bear on all the means and ends which enter into a human being's activities. In this way, it is a different kind of order from that which can be imposed on a man's activities by his decision to concentrate his energies on one objective. The single-mindedness of the lover of goodness is not the single-mindedness of the man with one big objective. Kierkegaard brings this out very well:

> For in truth there was a man on earth who seemed to will only one thing. It was unnecessary for him to insist upon it. Even if he had been silent about it, there were witnesses enough against him who testified now inhumanly he steeled his mind, how nothing touched him, neither tenderness, nor innocence, nor misery; how his blinded soul had eyes for nothing, and how the senses in him had only eyes for the one thing that he willed. And yet it was certainly a delusion, a terrible delusion, that he willed one thing. ([13] p. 49)

Such a man would have thought it inopportune, given certain situations, to continue pursuing his single end. And even if he had not, even if he pursued it to the end, the character of the pursuance would have marked it off from what Kierkegaard means by willing one thing.

Like Plato, Kierkegaard too sees the demands of goodness as eternal demands. They are not temporal considerations. By this he means that one cannot speak of a time to be good, without distortion. Kierkegaard says that 'a love of goodness will not belong to a certain section of life as fun and play belong to youth. It will not come and disappear as a whim or as a surprise' ([13]

p. 37). Thus, Kierkegaard wants to say, remorse and repentance are part of the eternal: they cannot be assigned a time. One cannot decide when to feel remorse or when to repent as if they were interests or desires to be placed in an order of priority or convenience. One cannot decide to repent at the eleventh hour. To make repentance a matter of convenient timing is not to repent. Kierkegaard wants to say that when one repents, it is always the eleventh hour: 'But repentance and remorse belong to the eternal in a man. And in this way each time that repentance comprehends guilt it understands that the eleventh hour has come' ([13] p. 36). For Kierkegaard, then, to speak of man's acquaintance with the eternal is, so far, to speak of his acquaintance with a love of goodness. This being so, we can see why it would be foolish to speak of eternal life as some kind of appendage to human existence, something which happens *after* human life on earth is over. Eternal life is the reality of goodness, that in terms of which human life is to be assessed. The difference between the man who aspired to eternal life in this sense and a man who did not would not be the difference between a man who did think he would live on after death and a man who did not think that he would live on after death. The difference would show in the attitudes they had to their respective lives. In one man, his desires and appetites would be, or would be aimed at being, subordinate to moral considerations, while in the other they would reign unchecked. Just as in the case of determining the state of a man's soul, so in the case of determining whether someone has a regard for the eternal, what needs to be examined is the kind of life he is living. As Kierkegaard says, 'the story of . . . life must once again have been wholly different in order to express continually immortality's difference from all the changeableness and the different kinds of variations of the perishable' ([13] p. 31). Given this context in which one kind of talk about eternal life and immortality has its home, one can see how speculations about continued existence after death are beside the point. Philosophical discussions of the immortality of the soul can now be something other than attempts to *find out* whether we do or do not live on after death; they can be attempts to appreciate the contexts in which talk about eternal life has moral and religious significance. The problem will no longer be seen in the way Flew describes it:

And if this future life is supposed to last for ever, then clearly the question whether or not it is fictitious (and if it is not, the consequent problem of ensuring that we shall pass it agreeably) is of quite overwhelming importance. For what are three-score years and ten compared with all eternity? ([4] p. 267)

Here, for Flew, eternity is a matter of duration, a matter of *more* life. He is able to bring a quantitative measure to show that eternity is infinitely longer than three-score years and ten. But as we have seen, the use of immortality we have been considering cuts right across this way of talking. Eternity is not an extension of this present life, but a mode of judging it. Eternity is not *more* life, but this life seen under certain moral and religious modes of thought. This is precisely what seeing this life *sub specie aeternitatis* would amount to. Is not this one of the reasons why Wittgenstein said:

> Not only is there no guarantee of the temporal immortality of the human soul, that is to say of its eternal survival after death; but, in any case, this assumption completely fails to accomplish the purpose for which it has always been intended. Or is some riddle solved by my surviving for ever? Is not this eternal life itself as much of a riddle as our present life? ([40] 6.4312)

What Wittgenstein shows here is that talk of eternal life need not enter human discourse in the way Flew assumes it does. Given the kind of role which Kierkegaard depicts the notion of the immortality of the soul as having, the postulation of a life after death would be neither here nor there, since the same questions about the character of *that* life would arise. Questions about the immortality of the soul are seen not to be questions concerning the extent of a man's life, and in particular concerning whether that life can extend beyond the grave, but questions concerning the kind of life a man is living.

And yet, important though I think these conclusions are, they are insufficient as an analysis of *religious* conceptions of eternal life and the immortality of the soul. The reason why this is so is because to talk of the demands of decency as eternal demands is not to specify the content of those demands. It is rather to mark them off in logical grammar from prudential considerations or considerations of convenience. But if this is the case, the adjective 'eternal' could apply in this context to a number of radically *different* moral conceptions. It is not that what we have said about immortality and eternal life does not apply to religious belief; it

49

does. The point is that it applies to much else too, so that the task now facing us is to say something further about specifically *religious* conceptions of immortality and eternity.

The religious notions of eternity and immortality I have in mind are closely connected with the idea of overcoming death. But what does overcoming death mean? As Flew points out, many different answers can be given in answer to this question. He suggests that it might be said that we overcome death because the influence of the evil and sometimes the good that we do lives on after us. Or it might be said that we overcome death because we live on in our descendants. It is not too difficult to think of other examples. A man may think that the only way to achieve immortality is to win a place in history, or to be remembered for one's artistic creations. Again, immortality might mean the kind of moral attitudes I have been trying to outline in this chapter. Eternal life would mean living and dying in a way which could not be rendered pointless by death. 'Our love is eternal', two people might say, although they know their love must end. The same might be said of friendship, and these phrases need not be empty. The difference between all these answers and the religious ones I want to discuss is that they do not involve 'turning towards the eternal' in the way that is expressed in Christianity (cf. [26] p. 126).

In turning away from the temporal to the eternal, the believer is said to attain immortality and to overcome death. All these notions hang very much together, and in talking about one one soon finds oneself talking about the other. In order to see in what sense the believer talks of overcoming death it is essential to think of him speaking in the first person. We have already noted that we cannot say the same where our deaths are concerned as we can say when we are talking about the deaths of other people. (1) The deaths of other people are events in our world, and can be analysed without remainder in those terms. But a complete analysis of my own death cannot be given in these terms. My own death is not an event in my world, but the end of my world, and as such its relation to me is radically different from the various relations in which other people's deaths stand to me. The fear of death when that death is my own death is necessarily different from the fear of another's death, however strong that latter fear may be. The fear of my own death is fear of my extinction as a person. I may be able to face the thought of any number of deaths, and yet be unable to face the thought of my own death. All the factual knowledge I possess about death as a clinical phenomenon does not help me to come to terms with the certain knowledge that I too shall die. We are now in the region which MacKinnon was hinting at as the region which goes beyond what the clinician can say about death (see [14]). (2) Even if Ivan Ilych's doctor had been more forth-coming, no amount of information would have made any difference to his problem in facing death. For what terrified Ivan Ilych was not the way in which he might die, but *that he had to die*. And although he knew, as all men know, that all men have to die, yet he did not know, in that he had not faced the fact, that *he* had to die. Tolstoy brings out such a state of mind vividly:

> The syllogism he had learnt from Kiezewetter's Logic: 'Caius is a man, men are mortal, therefore Caius is mortal', had always seemed to him correct as applied to Caius, but certainly not as applied to himself. That Caius – man in the abstract – was mortal, was perfectly correct, but he was not Caius, not an abstract man, but a creature quite quite separate from all others. He had been little Vanya, with a mamma and a papa, with Mitya and Volodya, with the toys, a coachman and a nurse, afterwards with Katenka and with all the joys, griefs, and delights of childhood, boyhood, and youth. What did Caius know of the smell of that striped leather ball Vanya had been so fond of? Had Caius kissed his mother's hand like that, and did the silk of her dress rustle so for Caius? Had he rioted like that at school when the pastry was bad? Had Caius been in love like that? Could Caius preside at a session as he did? 'Caius really was mortal, and it was right for him to die; but for me, little Vanya, Ivan Ilych, with all my thoughts and emotions, it's altogether a different matter. It cannot be that I ought to die. That would be too terrible.'
> Such was his feeling.
> 'If I had to die like Caius I should have known it was so. An inner voice would have told me so, but there was nothing of the sort in me and I and all my friends felt that our case was quite different from that of Caius. And now here it is!' he said to himself. 'It can't be. It's impossible! But here it is. How is this? How is one to understand it?' ([31] pp. 44–5)

Simply to be in such a state, to recognise as never before the reality of one's own death, is not, of course, religious in itself. The realisation may terrorise and paralyse one. It may be true, how-ever, that such a realisation is often a necessary precondition of

51

religious belief. It often involves an attitude which is the anti-thesis of religious faith, and from which the believer has to turn in order to believe. The attitude I have in mind is typified by Ivan Ilych. He was the centre of his world, and thought that only his fortunes and misfortunes were the real fortunes and misfortunes. His reputation in the eyes of others was all-important to him, and he felt that a worthy and enviable reputation could be attained solely by his own efforts. Death revealed to him the foolishness and falsity of such an attitude. But this attitude is hard to give up because it permeates so much of human thought. Simone Weil describes it as a certain kind of energy which human beings need to keep going:

> When we have enjoyed something for a long time, we think that it is ours, and that we are entitled to expect fate to let us go on enjoying it. Then there is the right to a compensation for every effort, be it work, suffering or desire. Every time that we put forth some effort and the equivalent of this effort does not come back to us in the form of some visible fruit, we have a sense of false balance and emptiness which makes us think that we have been cheated. ([34] p. 150)

Simone Weil illustrates how this desire for a certain equilibrium in life can be found in the good we do and in the evil we suffer:

> The effort of suffering from some offence causes us to expect the punishment or apologies of the offender, the effort of doing good makes us expect the gratitude of the person we have helped, but these are only particular cases of a universal law of the soul. Every time we give anything out we have an absolute need that at least the equivalent should come into us, and because we need this we think we have a right to it. Our debtors comprise all beings and all things; they are the entire universe. We think we have claims everywhere. In every claim which we think we possess there is always the idea of an imaginary claim of the past on the future. This is the claim which we have to renounce. ([34] pp. 150–1)

This renunciation is what the believer means by dying to the self. He ceases to see himself as the centre of his world. Death's lesson for the believer is to force him to recognise what all his natural instincts want to resist, namely, that he has no claims on the way

52

things go. Most of all, he is forced to realise that his own life is not a necessity. This again has been beautifully expressed by Simone Weil:

> The principal claim which we think we have on the universe is that our personality should continue. This claim implies all the others. The instinct of self-preservation makes us feel this continuation to be a necessity, and we believe that a necessity is a right. We are like the beggar who said to Talleyrand: 'Sir, I must live,' and to whom Talleyrand replied, 'I do not see the necessity for that.' Our personality is entirely dependent on external circumstances which have unlimited power to crush it. But we would rather die than admit this. From our point of view the equilibrium of the world is a combination of circumstances so ordered that our personality remains intact and seems to belong to us. All the circumstances of the past which have wounded our personality appear to us to be disturbances of balance which should infallibly be made up for one day or another by phenomena having a contrary effect. We live on the expectation of these compensations. The near approach of death is horrible chiefly because it forces the knowledge upon us that these compensations will never come. ([34] p. 151)

How then is death overcome? It is easy to think that it is overcome by escaping its clutches, as it were. By reducing the status of death to the status of sleep, we hope to wake again to a new and better life. But then the lesson religious believers see in death is lost, since death no longer reveals the fact that there is to be no compensation, but is seen as an additional fact for which compensation must be sought. That is why Simone Weil says that 'Belief in immortality is harmful because it is not in our power to conceive of the soul as really incorporeal. So this belief is in fact a belief in the prolongation of life, and it robs death of its purpose' ([35] p. 33). But need immortality mean this? We can agree with Simone Weil that 'The thought of death calls for a counterweight, and this counterweight – apart from grace – cannot be anything but a lie' ([35] p. 16), but nevertheless show how an account of immortality can be given in terms of grace. Such an account can be arrived at by displaying the contrast between the desire for compensation and the religious conception of dying to the self. This is the contrast between the temporal (that is, the concern with the self), and the eternal (that is, the concern with self-renunciation).

To speak in this latter way, however, is misleading, since a concern *with* self-renunciation would be self-defeating. The immortality of the soul cannot be *the object* of a person's strivings without being idolatrous. Simone Weil says:

> We must not help our neighbour *for* Christ but *in* Christ. May the self disappear in such a way that Christ can help our neighbour through the medium of our soul and body. May we be the slave whom his master sends to bear help to someone in misfortune. The help comes from the master, but it is intended for the sufferer. Christ did not suffer for his Father. He suffered for men by the Father's will. ([35] p. 40)

The soul which is rooted in the mortal is the soul where the ego is dominant in the way which Simone Weil describes in such penetrating detail in her works. The immortality of the soul by contrast refers to a person's relation to the self-effacement and love of others involved in dying to the self. Death is overcome in that dying to the self is the meaning of the believer's life. As Plato says, 'If this is true, and they have actually been looking forward to death all their lives, it would of course be absurd to be troubled when the thing comes for which they have so long been preparing and looking forward' ([21] 64A). When Ivan Ilych is able to die to his self-centredness and see other people as the creatures of God in love, he too sees that death is vanquished:

> 'It is finished!' said someone near him.
> He heard these words and repeated them in his soul.
> 'Death is finished,' he said to himself. 'It is no more!'
> He drew in a breath, stopped in the midst of a sigh, stretched out, and died. ([31] p. 73)

There is no contradiction in the way Tolstoy expresses the end of Ivan's life. Ivan says that death is no more, and the next moment he dies. Yet I repeat: there is no contradiction. Of course, if one will not allow that overcoming death can mean anything other than prolongation of life after death, then Ivan dies deluded. But if one sees that this is not all it can mean, and appreciates the kind of exposition Simone Weil gives, one can also see how it can be said that although Ivan Ilych died, death had no dominion over him.

I am suggesting then, that eternal life for the believer is participation in the life of God, and that this life has to do with dying to the self, seeing that all things are a gift from God, that nothing is ours by right or necessity. At this point, however, many philosophers will say that I have yet to prove the existence of God. To speak of self-renunciation, as Simone Weil does, as an imitation of the act of divine self-renunciation at creation and on the Cross (notice the contrast between this and the God of power of the second chapter) is not to prove the existence of the divine subject who so renounces himself. To speak of the love of God is not to prove the existence of a God of love. To say that everything is a gift from God is not to prove the existence of the Giver. I believe these popular philosophical objections to be radically misconstrued. In learning by contemplation, attention, renunciation, what forgiving, thanking, loving, etc. mean in these contexts, the believer is participating in the reality of God; *this is what we mean by God's reality*.

This reality is independent of any given believer, but its independence is not the independence of a separate biography. It is independent of the believer in that the believer measures his life against it. Here, it is necessary to note an ambiguity in our use of the notion of immortality. Sometimes the term is used to refer to a particular relation of the individual to the reality of God, namely one of attention, love, striving, etc. But the term is also used to indicate the relation of a person to God, no matter what that relation may be. Thus, a man's immortal soul may be in a state of damnation. It is important to remember that the community of believers is wider than the community of worshippers. Those who believe in God include not only those who love him, but also those who hate him, are afraid of him, rebel against him, try to be rid of him, etc. etc. The relation between God and the individual varies accordingly. The believer may ask God to turn his wrath away from him. But here, what his prayer comes to is not, as Geach's analysis would lead us to suppose, 'Don't do that to me', but rather, 'Don't let me become that'; that is, 'Don't let me become the sort of person whose life is devoid of love towards God' (cf. [18] p. 51). The immortality of the soul refers to the state an individual is in in relation to the unchanging reality of God. It is in this way that the notions of the immortality of the soul and of eternal life go together.

'But', someone might say, 'all this tells us something only about the relation of an individual to God during this present life. It says nothing of the destiny of the soul after death, and since this is an essential part of what has been meant by the immortality of the soul, the offered account is inadequate.' I want to show that this criticism is misplaced, that what I have said does justice not only to what might be meant by the relation of the soul to the eternal in this life, but also to what might be meant by the eternal destiny of the soul after death. This can be brought out by considering the way in which what I want to call 'eternal predicates' can be ascribed to the dead (cf. [18] pp. 41 f.).

This latter notion is not easy to grasp. It is best approached by contrasting it with its opposite, namely, the way in which we normally ascribe predicates to people. Despite the diversity and disagreement often involved, we do have criteria which determine when it is appropriate to call a man angry, pleased, contented, apprehensive, etc. etc. And there are limits, however loosely drawn, which, if transgressed, make us wonder what is being said. If a man has longed for a certain job, for example, has constantly expressed how pleased and contented he would be if he could get it, we do not know what to make of him if we find him indignant on hearing of his appointment. If this were how he behaved generally, we should say that he is unable to see the kind of bearing that things have on each other. Of course, a certain background may be provided in which his indignation becomes intelligible. He may find out that he has not been appointed because of his merits, but because it suited someone's plans to have him occupy that post, or his former attitude to the post may have been a case of self-deception, and so on. This, however, merely serves to underline my point, namely, that there are criteria which govern our ascription of predicates to other people. The important feature of such predicates for our present purposes is that they are essentially temporal in character. By this I simply mean that the vast majority of predicates we ascribe to people belong to them for a certain time. Consider, for example: 'I was angry yesterday', 'He became quite hysterical when he heard the news', etc. The reason why the predicates we ascribe to people change is quite simple: change is a central characteristic of human life

We also ascribe predicates to people when we make judgements of character which indicate their dominant characteristics throughout a changing course of events or throughout all their lives. Consider: 'He was courageous to the end' or 'He never let things get him down', and so on. Indeed in the case of certain strong characters we often say that they never change. The same could be said of stubborn characters too. But even though they do not change in fact, this does not mean that the predicates ascribed to them are not temporal predicates, since it still makes sense to suppose that they might change. One might say, 'My father could never be sadistic'; one is not prepared to say that he could ever be sadistic in the future. But when we say that it makes sense to say that the father will change, we are not making a prediction about what will in fact happen, but commenting on what it makes sense to say in such contexts; we are commenting on the logic of predication.

The predicates we ascribe to each other, then, are temporal; people change. And, of course, we often change each other. We can argue with the opinions of the living, and often do. This is the case even when the people with whom we are arguing are those for whom we have a deep regard. Consider, for example, disputes between parents and children. Parents may express the wish that their son marries at a certain time, takes up a certain job, or lives at a certain place. The son may hold out against them, arguing that it is important that he should be allowed to make up his own mind on such issues. The point is that it makes sense to argue against the will of the living in the hope of changing it.

Things are very different in the case of the will of the dead. The will of the dead cannot be changed; it is fixed and unchanging. Here, the predicates are eternal predicates. When a man dies, what he is, the state of his soul, is fixed forever. There are no acts of volition, no developments, among the dead. For the believer, his eternal destiny at death is determined by his relationship to God.

It will be objected that the analysis of the notion of eternal destiny being offered does not do justice to Christian beliefs in the community of the dead. Geach says that 'if there is no resurrection', meaning by this survival after death, 'it is superfluous and vain to pray for the dead'. This certainly does not follow. To begin with, prayers for the dead may change the status of the dead *in God*, which is the only way the status of the dead can change. By the living praying for the souls of the departed, the relationship between the living and the dead in God is changed. Since God's activity in this context is to be understood in terms of his spirit at work in the prayers of believers, it makes sense to speak of the prayers of the living changing the status of the dead in God's eyes. ([18] p. 128). There may well be many religious disagreements about the appropriateness of such prayers, and about the occasions on which they can and cannot be said. St Augustine in his dissertation on 'The Divination of Demons and Care For The Dead' distinguishes between those souls whose status cannot be changed by prayers because they do not need such help or because their earthly lives place them beyond the possibility of such help on the one hand, and those souls whose earthly lives show that such prayers could change their status in God. (3) Here, what is important to note is that what it makes sense to say about the dead in petitionary prayers is determined, to a large extent, by the relation of the dead to God when they were alive.

Of course, not all prayers relating to the dead are petitionary. Some are contemplative. The contrast we have already drawn between temporal predicates and eternal predicates should help us to understand these. The will of the dead cannot be changed, but it can be made an object of contemplation. Such contemplation of a loved one, let us say, who is now dead can be an act of self-examination and reappraisal. In this respect, the will of the dead is akin to the will of God; it is the measure in terms of which the individual assesses himself or understands himself and the world. (4)

It might be thought that if the prayers of the living for the dead pose problems for the way in which I have argued, the prayers of the dead for the living pose even greater problems. This is not the case. Surely, one might think, if the dead are said to pray for the living, this must imply some kind of duration after death, another existence in which certain activities are carried on, namely, prayers for the living. This way of reasoning assumes that when we ascribe prayers to the dead, prayer must mean what it means when the living pray. We need to remind ourselves, however, of the contrast we drew between temporal and eternal predicates. If the dead pray for us, we cannot equate such prayers with the prayers of the living. The prayers of the dead are prayers *from or in eternity*. We cannot ask of them questions which are appropriate to ask of the prayers of the living: Were they verbal prayers or silent prayers? How long did they last? Were they said with difficulty or easily? and so on. The activity of the dead is the activity of the eternal in them. What is more, the possibility of this activity again depends on the extent to which the eternal was in their lives when they were alive. It is because of the presence of the eternal in the life of the Virgin Mary and of the saints that they, though dead, can yet speak. Van Antwerp brings out this point well by reference to St Augustine:

But the martyrs? We *know* that they are interested in the affairs of the living because the prayers of those who ask them for favours are answered, and requests are granted through their intercession. Does not this prove that the dead *are* interested in

58

the affairs of the living? Augustine uses an example to demonstrate this, which would be very familiar to the addressee of the letter, Paulinus: the appearance of the patron St Felix, answering the prayers of the people of Nola at the time of the siege. No, says Augustine, even this must be considered not as a natural work of the dead, but as miraculous, for 'the dead, through their own power, are not able to be interested in the acts of the living'. These miraculous acts do happen, but it is 'through the divine power that the martyrs are interested in the acts of the living'. ([1] p. 36)

Augustine gets into difficulties over *how* the martyrs can help. He wonders whether they are actually present or whether they work through angelic ministrations. I am suggesting that in order to reach a philosophical understanding of the notion of the eternal speaking through the dead, we need to take the religious community into account and the status of the dead in that community. This can be underlined by reference to the special days given to saints and martyrs. Understood superficially and superstitiously, it might appear that what is being said is that these dead people are more active on these days than on others, readier to listen to the pleas of the living, more amenable to persuasion, and so on. But all this misses the point. The point of such special days, though no doubt frequently distorted and misused, is first, to concentrate worship at a particular time in a certain context; that is, it can be seen as a devotional discipline. Second, the days are *special* days because of something which happened on the day in the life of the saint: his birth, his death, his martyrdom, his teachings, and so on. That being so, it is natural to think on these things with a special degree of effort on such days.

We have seen that neither prayers for the dead nor the prayers of the dead become superfluous notions if one refuses to equate eternal life with a prolongation of life after death. The main context of eternal life we have considered, however, is not one where the dead become sources of sustenance for the living. There is an important anonymity in Christianity, which means that immortality of the soul is not a matter of immortal fame. Eternal life is not to be known of men but to be known of God. It is in this sense that every sparrow that falls is known. The dead who die in him are said to be blessed because to die in such a way is to die at peace with man and God and to be beyond the reach of death's dominion.

Before ending this chapter, let us allow the by now familiar objection to rear its head once again. Someone may say that if the philosophical analysis of the notion of immortality I have attempted to give is anywhere near the truth, the whole notion is an illusion. He may say that there is no difference between the man who does and the man who does not believe in the life eternal: death is the end of both of them. Neither are going to survive their deaths. This is true, but why should we assume that the difference between a believer and an unbeliever consists in this? The objector may see no point in living according to God's commands unless there is such a difference. In that case, we are back to the desire for compensation. When Jesus saw men eaten up by pride, he said that they have their reward; that is, that is all their lives amount to; they are wedded to the temporal. But the objector wants a further eternal punishment, otherwise he thinks that the proud man has got away with it. But what has he got away with? If the objector is not careful, he will find himself talking of a good time which has to be paid for later. But the believer does not describe such a way of living as a good time, but as sickness of soul. For a person to die unaware of his distance from God would not, for the believer, be a matter of that person escaping anything, but of his dying in the worst possible state. For the believer, his death, like his life, is to be in God. For him, this is the life eternal which death cannot touch; the immortality which finally places the soul beyond the reach of the snares and temptations of this mortal life.

4 Immortality and Truth

This essay began by posing the question 'Does belief in immortality rest on a mistake?' I suggested that this question is itself based on a mistake, a mistake concerning what are taken to be necessary presuppositions of a belief in immortality. In the last chapter I attempted to show how an alternative account of immortality is possible. Yet, even if philosophers were disposed to accept such an account, they might still want to ask, 'But is it true?' Before ending this essay, therefore, it is necessary to enquire what 'truth' amounts to in the context of belief in the immortality of the soul.

Supposing someone asks whether a belief in the immortality of the soul is true or not, what might this question mean? In the light of the arguments of the last chapter, we can see that the question of truth in this context has little to do with verifying whether a future state of affairs, namely, the continued existence of people after death, is to take place. Many contemporary philosophers of religion feel, however, that if the question of the truth of a belief in the immortality of the soul is divorced from such considerations, the belief has been robbed of all its vital significance. These philosophers feel that the belief entails the fulfilment of what Professor Wisdom has called 'the logically unique expectation', namely, that we shall have experiences after death (see [39]). Furthermore, they feel that if religious believers were told that belief in immortality was divorced from such an expectation and independent of it, the belief would lose its hold on them immediately. On the other hand, these same philosophers are often prepared to admit that belief in the immortality of the soul contains far more than what is contained in the logically unique expectation. They recognise that the belief is bound up with a whole attitude towards the world, for example, the view of the body as the prison of the soul.

The philosophers I have in mind, however, stress that no matter what 'extra' elements are involved in belief in the immortality of the soul, they are all dependent on the factual truth of survival after death. In other words, if the latter cannot be established, it becomes pointless to enquire into the meaning of the other elements in the belief. This point of view is well illustrated by one of Professor Flew's papers on the subject. Flew admits that as far as the wider context of belief in the immortality of the soul is concerned, his 'paper does not even begin to come to grips with this sort of complex of belief and attitude of which utterances about the immortality of the soul form a part' ([7] p. 247 n.). But one has the strong impression in reading Flew that he is not unduly worried by this fact. On his view there is no reason why such complexities should be discussed. If it makes no sense to talk of survival after death, why bother to discuss complex attitudes which entail such survival? Flew justifies these philosophical omissions by saying that 'it is worth pointing out that, rightly or wrongly, most people who held such faiths have believed that the '"logically unique expectation"' was in fact justified: and would be no longer able or willing (psychologically) to maintain their faiths if convinced that it was not' ([7] p. 247 n.). A philosopher who thinks that Flew's criticisms of the intelligibility of survival after death are irrelevant as far as the immortality of the soul is concerned, nevertheless agrees with this latter comment. W. H. Poteat says, 'I think it is important to recognise that the overwhelming majority of people in the contemporary world, Christian and non-Christian, take the essence of the Christian claim (as Flew seems to do) to be a belief to the effect that 'I will survive my death'; and further, that they are culturally conditioned by the same forces which induce Flew to take as his paradigm for meaningful discourse the language we use about the common-sense world; and finally that on their own premises, Flew's demonstration of the contradictoriness of 'I will survive my death' must be devastating. If 'death' is the kind of concept which he holds that it is, then to speak of surviving it *is* utter nonsense' ([23] pp. 209–10). I believe that the issue of the relations between believers and the accounts they give of their beliefs are far more complex than either Flew or Poteat recognise. This is not a peripheral matter; since ignoring such complexity leads to an obscuring of what 'truth' means in these contexts.

The above conclusion needs justifying. Let us consider one of Flew's own examples. In his paper on 'Death', Flew expresses misgivings that D. M. MacKinnon, his fellow symposiast, is in danger of excluding the would-be factual claims involved when he discusses the notion of immortality. Flew's misgivings are expressed in terms of the belief that 'we shall all meet again beyond the grave', and this is the example I want to consider. Flew says that although this hope 'is also expressive of so much else of agony and hope, essentially and fundamentally it makes a would-be factual claim that the logically unique expectation is justified. It is through this alone that it can console the grief of the bereaved: not by some general assurance that all will be well, for for him without the beloved nothing will be well again; but by its particular implication that one day they may both be reunited in a world to come' ([4] p. 269). It is clear how Flew would argue. First, he insists that what is essential in the belief that we all meet beyond the grave is the expectation that at some future time, after death, such a meeting will take place. Second, Flew says that any other elements present in the belief are secondary to the above expectation. Third, since the expectation is unintelligible, there is no need to be unduly worried by the fact that the other elements have not been given much attention. Fourth, the primary importance of the expectation is shown by the fact that only its fulfilment would bring comfort to a person who expresses the belief that we shall all meet beyond the grave. So if someone says that we shall all meet again beyond the grave, Flew and many other philosophers would respond by asking, 'And *do* we meet again beyond the grave?' The answer clearly is, 'No, we do not.' Probably, one should also add, 'And it isn't at all clear what could be meant by saying that we shall all meet again beyond the grave.' Thus, the falsity or unintelligibility of belief in immortality is demonstrated. I want to argue that this analysis of the religious belief in question is too unimaginative and by ignoring complexities, obscures meaning.

It might be said, however, that the alleged complexities are of the philosopher's making, and that matters are really as straightforward as Flew claims them to be. In another of his papers Flew considers the argument of those who have said that life after death is intelligible because it is imaginable. Since a man could imagine witnessing his own funeral, it at least makes sense to suppose that he might witness his own funeral. Flew denies this. He says that while it is easy enough to imagine one's funeral, it is impossible to imagine oneself witnessing one's funeral. Flew says:

> If it really is I who witness it then it is not my funeral but only 'my funeral' (in inverted commas): and if it really is my funeral then I cannot be a witness, for I shall be dead and in the coffin. ([7] p. 246)

63

But what if someone says he can imagine all this?

> Surely I can perfectly well imagine my own funeral, really my own funeral with my body in the coffin and not a substitute corpse or a weight of bricks; with me there watching it all, but invisible, intangible, a disembodied spirit? Well, yes, this seems all right: until someone asks the awkward question 'Just how does all this differ from your imagining your own funeral without your being there at all (except as the corpse in the coffin)?'

What Flew does is to consider the picture of a man witnessing his own funeral and press for answers to questions which he thinks show the logical inadequacy of the picture. Flew never asks himself whether he *ought* to press for answers to the questions he asks. He never asks himself whether these pictures are pictures *of* anything. He assumes that they are, indeed, that they must be. He then has the relatively easy task of showing the logical contradictoriness of that which these pictures are supposed to be pictures of.

But should the pictures be submitted to the kind of pressure Flew brings to bear on them? Might it not be the case that in treating religious pictures in this way one is uprooting them from their natural setting? In his lectures on belief Wittgenstein comments on the fact that the word 'God' is amongst the earliest learnt. It is learnt through pictures, catechisms, etc. 'But', Wittgenstein says, 'not the same consequences as with pictures of aunts. I wasn't shown [that which the picture pictured]' ([42] p. 59). But this is precisely the way in which Flew wants to deal with religious pictures. If a man says that he can imagine himself witnessing his funeral, Flew replies that this must be a mistake. Either the man is not witnessing his funeral or it is not he who is witnessing it. Similarly, if people say that they shall all meet after death, Flew can bring to bear on this alleged prediction all the logical difficulties we have considered in this essay. But when people say such things what do they mean? No doubt some are in the state of confusion Flew takes them to be in, but this is not true in every case. It must be remembered that the very same people who say that God is in heaven would treat as trivial the question why the astronauts have not so much as caught a glimpse of him. Might it not be also true that the people who say that they can imagine themselves witnessing their own funerals would treat as boringly uninteresting the question how one person can be in two places at the same time? Or consider Wittgenstein's comment on the example ' "God's eye sees everything" – I want to say of this that it uses a picture . . . what conclusions are you going to draw? etc. Are eyebrows going to be talked of, in connection with the Eye of God?' ([42] p. 71). In so far as he thinks that we cannot imagine ourselves witnessing our own funerals, Flew is like a man who every time he hears God's eye mentioned, insists on talking about God's eyebrows. The pictures were not meant to be used in this way.

But how are the pictures to be used? There is no general answer to this question, but one can offer some examples. Consider the visitations which Ebenezer Scrooge is depicted as experiencing on that fateful Christmas eve in his life. In particular, think of how he sees himself led by the Ghost of Christmas Yet To Come.

> The spirit stood among the graves, and pointed down to one. He [Scrooge] advanced towards it, trembling. The phantom was exactly as it had been, but he dreaded that he saw new meaning in its solemn shape. . . . Scrooge crept towards it, trembling as he went; and following the finger, read upon the stone of the neglected grave his own name, EBENEZER SCROOGE. ([3] pp. 87–8)

Professor Flew would no doubt object. But what is he objecting to? Perhaps the fact that it is logically impossible to imagine Scrooge both looking at his grave and yet being buried in it. And, of course, once one begins to press the picture in those directions, it becomes impossible. But why not remain with the original role of the picture? As Dickens depicts the matter, the role of these visions in Scrooge's life is a means of reflecting on his life as a whole. Now, while alive, he can think of his death and events after his death in a certain way, a way which reorientates his whole way of living. This is brought out vividly in the picture of Scrooge seeing his own deserted and violated corpse on his bed and seeing his own uncared-for grave. If a man insisted on forcing this picture in directions which would bring out its contradications, he would be misunderstanding and misusing the picture. Perhaps he would want to say that the picture is not literally true. But in what sense is Dickens's story only figuratively true? 'Just because it is a story' someone might say. But it is easy enough to think of someone actually giving an account of his conversion in terms used by Ebenezer Scrooge. What then? Is this still not literally true? But what is literal truth in this context? When we say that something is not literally true, we can compare it with the context where it *could* be literally true. But we are agreed that this is what cannot be done in the cases I am considering. When we try to say what it would be like for a person to look at his own grave, to witness his own funeral, or to meet his friends after death, we find ourselves using words devoid of meaning. So we have no original context of literal truth which the religious pictures can distort or deviate from. Once we realise this we are more likely to consider the use of the pictures themselves. If we want to speak of 'literal truth' here, might we not say that the literal truth is precisely the relation of Scrooge to the visions he experienced and the role they played in changing his whole way of life? (1) We can look again at Flew's question when he asks what is the difference between imagining oneself witnessing one's funeral and simply imagining one's funeral. The answer can be found in the fact that one's presence as observer in the religious picture is an expression of how a person can reflect on his life as a whole or how a person, now, can reflect on events which will occur after his death. I am not considering whether such a picture *ought* to be an expression of such reflection; I am simply noting the fact that it *is*, whereas simply imagining one's funeral need not be connected with any form of reflection on one's life. The same is true of the belief that we shall all meet again beyond the grave. Such a picture may itself be an expression of the belief that people should act towards each other, not according to the status and prestige that people have acquired or failed to acquire, during the course of their lives, but as children of God, in the equality which death will reveal. A similar picture of judgement is found at the end of the *Gorgias*:

Now in the days of Cronos there existed a law respecting the destiny of man, which has always been, and still continues to be in Heaven, – that he who has lived all his life in justice and holiness shall go, when he dies, to the Islands of the Blessed, and dwell there in perfect happiness out of the reach of evil; but that he who has lived unjustly and impiously shall go to the house of vengeance and punishment, which is called Tartarus. And in the time of Cronos, and even later in the reign of Zeus, the judgement was given on the very day on which the men were to die; the judges were alive, and the men were alive; and the consequence was that the judgements were not well given. Then Pluto and the authorities from the Islands of the Blessed came to Zeus, and said that the souls found their way to the wrong places. Zeus said: 'I shall put a stop to this; the judgements are not well given, and the reason is that the judged have their clothes on, for they are alive; and there are many having evil souls who are apparelled in fair bodies, or wrapt in wealth or rank, and when the day of judgement arrives many witnesses come forward and witness on their behalf that they have lived righteously. The judges are awed by them, and they themselves too have their clothes on when judging; their eyes and ears and their whole bodies are interposed as a veil before their own souls. All this is a hindrance to them; there are clothes of the judges and clothes of the judged. – What is to be done? I will tell you:– In the first place, I will deprive men of the foreknowledge of death, which they at present possess; that is a commission, of which I have already entrusted the execution to Prometheus: in the second place, they shall be entirely stripped before they are judged, for they shall be judged when they are dead; then the judge too shall be naked, that is to say, dead: he with his naked soul shall pierce into the other naked soul, and they shall die suddenly and be deprived of all their kindred, and leave their brave attire strewn upon the earth; conducted in this manner, the judgement will be just.' ([20] 523)

Here, too, we have the use of a picture. Flew says that we understand the myths, but we do not expect such things to happen ([4] pp. 267–8). But to say one does not expect such things to happen is to show that one has not understood the myth. The myth is not a prediction that certain things are going to happen, but is itself the expression and embodiment of a reflection on, or vision of, the meaning of life and death. Rush Rhees says that

In his notes on Frazer, Wittgenstein speaks of the impressiveness that the rites of earlier peoples may have for us. 'When Frazer begins by telling the story of the forest-king of Nemi, he does this in a tone which shows that something strange and terrible is happening here. And that is the answer to the question 'why is this happening?': Because it is terrible. In other words, what strikes us in these proceedings as terrible, impressive, horrible, tragic, etc., anything but trivial and insignificant, *that* is what gave birth to them. . . . If we place the story of the priest-king of Nemi side by side with the expression 'the majesty of death', we see that they are one. The life of the priest-king represents what is meant by that expression. [43] pp. 235–6

It was because of a sense of 'the majesty of death' that the rite

67

itself had to be terrible. Sometimes, unless the symbol itself were sinister, we should not be alive to what was represented. ([24] pp. 152–3)

I am suggesting that similar points can be made about religious beliefs like belief in the Last Judgement, that the family will be one again in heaven, that we all live under the eye of God, and so on. What we find religiously and ethically impressive in these beliefs is what gave rise to them. *Believing* them has little in common with any kind of conjecture. It has to do with living by them, drawing sustenance from them, judging oneself in terms of them, being afraid of them, etc. Wittgenstein says:

Here believing obviously plays much more this role: suppose we said that a certain picture might play the role of constantly admonishing me, or I always think of it. Here, an enormous difference would be between those people for whom the picture is constantly in the foreground, and the others who just didn't use it at all.

Those who said: 'Well, possibly it may happen and possibly not' would be on an entirely different plane. ([42] p. 56)

Wittgenstein says that these pictures are unshakeable beliefs in the sense that they form the framework within which those who live by them assess themselves and the events that befall them. Consider again the example with which we began: the belief that we shall meet again beyond the grave. For Flew, the belief is shown to be confused by treating it as a prediction and by demonstrating the logical contradictoriness of what is predicted. I am suggesting that this procedure ignores the religious and ethical significance of the belief. A man may actually visualise his family, most of whom are dead, embracing each other in a reunion after death. Of course, awkward questions can be asked about whether they are really embracing each other, and if so what is one to make of the identity of the buried or cremated bodies. But these questions are not simply awkward, they are also trivial. The picture of the family reunion may have an ethical and religious role in the person's life, one which we have had reason to mention already. (2) The man may look on his relationship to his family as going beyond death, and his obligations to them as something which death cannot erase. The picture of the family reunion after death is not a prediction for which he has evidence, but a vision in terms of which

68

much of his own life is lived out. The picture is not assessed by appeal to evidence. On the contrary, the picture, for this man, is the measure of assessment. He subjects his own desires to those of the family, does what he thinks would be pleasing in their eyes, and so on. He cannot compromise with them, for they are dead. One can argue with the will of the living, but one cannot argue with the will of the dead. Any attempt to compromise with the will of the dead leads to a decline in the hold of the picture over one and in one's faith in the picture. Kierkegaard expresses the matter well with regard to the will of the dead when he says,

But the transfigured one exists only as transfigured, not visibly to the earthly eye, not audibly to the earthly ear, only in the sacredly still silence of shame. He cannot be changed, not in the least particular, without its being instantly noted, and without all being lost, and without his vanishing. ([13] p. 81)

There is no compromise with this religious picture; one either abides by it or loses it.

In the light of these remarks one can see, perhaps, why the relations between believers and the account they give of what they believe are more complex than Flew or Poteat suggest. (3) When a believer is asked by an unsympathetic philosopher to give an account of his beliefs, he already finds himself in a strange situation. He is being asked to assume an attitude towards his beliefs to which he is unaccustomed; that is, one of questioning, analysing and describing. Naturally, he turns his attention to the picture which is in the forefront of his thoughts, the picture, let us say, of the family reunion. What he does, however, is to ignore the natural setting of the picture in trying to meet the philosopher's questions. He feels that it is important to retain the picture, and yet in the light of the philosopher's probings the importance of the picture seems to elude him. Thus, we often find the believer agreeing with the philosopher's account of his belief – 'You *do* believe that we meet again beyond the grave don't you?' – and finding himself quite unable to meet the philosophical objections to the account. I am not saying that religious beliefs are never confused and that the philosophical objections never reflect what the believer believes. All I am saying is that very often the philosophical objections are irrelevant, and I have been offering a reason why the believer often does not recognise this irrelevance. Perhaps more often than not the believer's faith is a complex tangle of beliefs and confused accounts of those beliefs. What I wish to stress is the logical independence of the beliefs from the confusions attributed to believers by many philosophers.

In the course of this essay I have been trying to bring out the force of certain religious pictures, but it is not an easy matter. This is not simply because of lack of ability on my part, but also because of what these pictures are. The pictures are not poor substitutes for other ways of saying things. Often, there is no other or better way of stating what the pictures say. Wittgenstein says,

> Suppose someone, before going to China, when he might never see me again, said to me: 'We might see one another after death' – would I necessarily say that I don't understand him? I might say (want to say) simply, 'Yes, I *understand* him entirely.'
> *Lewy.* 'In this case, you might only mean that he expressed a certain attitude.'
> I would say 'No, it isn't the same as saying "I'm very fond of you" ' – and it may not be the same as saying anything else. It says what it says. Why should you be able to substitute anything else? ([42] pp. 70–1)

Earlier, discussing a similar example, Wittgenstein asks,

> How am I to find out whether this proposition is to be regarded as an empirical proposition – 'You'll see your dead friend again'? Would I say: 'He is a bit superstitious'? Not a bit.
> He might have been apologetic. (The man who stated it categorically was more intelligent than the man who was apologetic about it)....
> He always says it, but he doesn't make any search. He puts on a queer smile. 'His story had that dreamlike quality.' My answer would be in this case 'Yes', and a particular explanation. ([42] pp. 62–3)

The explanation, I take it, would be an attempt, however inadequate, to bring out the force of the religious picture. And when the force of such pictures is brought out, I suggest, we can see that they can be distinguished from hypotheses, conjectures or empirical propositions. It would be hard to find an adequate substitute for a song quoted by Tylor from a Ho dirge:

> We ever loved and cherished you; and have lived long together under the same roof; Desert it not now!... Come to your home!

70

It is swept for you and clean; and we are there who loved you ever; and there is rice put for you; and water; Come home, come home, come to us again! ([33] p. 33)

If someone asked, 'And did the departed spirit actually come home?' would not this be an example of a supremely foolish question? One might reply, although the reply would not be an answer but a rejection of the question, by saying that as long as people can sing the song the dead have not deserted them. The song is an expression of that truth. But it is unlikely that this reply would be understood by anyone who did not understand the song.

From a consideration of the kind of force which characteristic religious pictures have, we can see that to ask whether they are true as if they were would-be empirical propositions is to ask the wrong kind of question. It is of the utmost philosophical import-ance to recognise that for the believers these pictures constitute truths, truths which form the essence of life's meaning for them. To ask someone whether he thinks these beliefs are true is not to ask him to produce evidence for them, but rather to ask him whether he can live by them, whether he .can digest them, whether they constitute food for him. If the answer is in the affirmative then no doubt there will be factual consequences for him. If a man does believe that death has no dominion over the unity of the family, that the family are one in heaven, he will make decisions and react in ways very unlike the man who holds ideas such as that everyone has his own life to live, that the old have had their chance and should make way for the young, that no one should stand in anyone else's way, and so on. In this way, belief may not simply determine one's reactions to events that befall one, but actually determine what one takes the alternatives facing one to be. If a man asks, 'I wonder whether it's all true?' that question, if not confused, is not a request for a proof, but an expression of his doubt regarding whether there is anything in all this.

There is one well-known objection to the analysis of 'true religious beliefs' which I have offered which has lately gathered new momentum. The objection was expressed once by Flew as follows:

Suppose . . . we are in doubt as to what someone who gives vent to an utterance is asserting, or suppose that, more radically, we are sceptical as to whether he is really asserting anything at all, one way of trying to understand (or perhaps it will be to expose) his utterance is to attempt to find what he would regard as counting against, or as being incompatible with, its truth. For if the utterance is indeed an assertion, it will necessarily be equivalent to a denial of the negation of that assertion. And anything which would count against the assertion, or which would induce the speaker to withdraw it and to admit that it had been mistaken, must be part of (or the whole of) the meaning of the negation of that assertion. And to know the meaning of the negation of an assertion, is as near as makes no matter, to knowing the meaning of that assertion. And if there is nothing which a putative assertion denies then there is nothing which it asserts either: and so it is not really an assertion. ([5] p. 98)

It is clear how this objection would apply to what I have been saying. I have stressed that religious beliefs are truths for the believer rather than conjectures which are taken on trust because the evidence for them is not particularly strong. I have claimed that for the believer, the religious pictures I have mentioned are the means rather than the object of assessment. Flew wants to argue that if these pictures really say anything, then there must be something which would count against the alleged truth of what they say. I, on the other hand, want to argue that as a matter of fact many religious pictures cannot be understood in this way. They were not established by means of evidence and cannot be overthrown by means of evidence either. That is not to say that they cannot be overthrown, but that fact requires a different explanation in this context. Lately, Flew's objection has been reintroduced into recent discussion of this question by Kai Nielsen. He argues that it is not enough to claim, as I have done, that there are religious believers who live by religious pictures similar to those I have mentioned, since there are also people who have given up and turned their backs on these pictures. Nielsen says,

We should counterpose against the fact that religious language is a *fait accompli* another fact, namely, that at all times and at all places, even among the most primitive tribes, there have been sceptics and scoffers, people who though perfectly familiar with the religious language game played in their culture would not play religious language game, not because they could not, but because, even though they were perfectly familiar with it

72

even though they had an insiders' understanding of it, they found it incoherent. ([16] p. 196)

Notice that although Flew begins by saying that *one* way of finding out whether someone is saying something is to find out what would count against what he is saying, this quickly becomes for him the only test of whether religious truths are saying something or not. One finds a similar assumption in Nielsen's remarks. He assumes that the overthrow of a religious belief must consist in finding out that the evidence counts against it or that it is internally incoherent. Again, my aim is not to deny the existence of sceptics and scoffers, but to deny Nielsen's analysis of their activities. In doing so, however, an alternative account must be offered. I believe an alternative account is available, one which throws further light on the nature of religious belief.

In what way can religious pictures lose their hold on people's lives? Does the undeniable fact that they often do lose their hold mean that contrary evidence has been found which shows the picture to have been mistaken? Nielsen speaks of people who are perfectly familiar with religious beliefs but who do not hold them, but find them incoherent. This description covers a multitude of different cases and I can only mention a few.

Let us consider an account Tolstoy provides of how one man ceased to believe:

S., a clever and truthful man, once told me the story of how he ceased to believe. On a hunting expedition, when he was already twenty-six, he once, at the place where they put up for the night, knelt down in the evening to pray – a habit retained from childhood. His elder brother, who was at the hunt with him, was lying on some hay and watching him. When S. had finished and was settling down for the night, his brother said to him: 'So you still do that?'

They said nothing more to one another. But from that day S. ceased to say his prayers or go to church. And now he has not prayed or received communion, for thirty years. And this not because he knows his brother's convictions and has joined him in them, nor because he has decided anything in his own soul, but simply because a word spoken by his brother was like the push of a finger on a wall that was ready to fall by its own weight. The word only showed that where he thought there was faith, in reality there had long been an empty space, and that there-

73

fore the utterance of words and the making of signs of the cross and genuflections while praying were quite senseless actions. Becoming conscious of their senselessness he could not continue them. ([32] p. 5)

Tolstoy provides an excellent example here of *one* way in which religious pictures and practices can lose their hold on a man's life. There is no talk of weighing evidence, etc., but nevertheless there is talk of senselessness. What made the practices senseless for S. was precisely what they had become in his life, 'a habit retained from childhood'. That is all the practice of praying had become, a routine he went through before turning in at night. Tolstoy tells us explicitly that S. did not give up his beliefs because he weighed them up against his brother's convictions and found them wanting. Neither did he decide to give up his beliefs: He simply discovered, in the way Tolstoy describes, that the beliefs meant nothing to him. But what leads to such a discovery? I suggest that very often the answer is as follows. A religious picture loses its hold on a person's life because a rival picture wins his allegiance. The picture of the Last Judgement may lose its hold on a person because he has been won over by a rival secular picture. The other picture is a rival, not because it shows that the original picture is a mistake, but because if it is operative in a person's life, the very character of its claims excludes the religious picture. The individual's attention is now focused on a new picture and his energies are spent in that direction. I do not suggest that this is what happened in Tolstoy's example. There, it is more likely that the character of the religious practices had never developed and that the routine was carried out in a context of indifference. The practice was not nourished by other aspects of S.'s life but was independent of them.

The point of interest for us, however, is to consider what might happen when someone gives an account of religious beliefs in such circumstances, that is, when his attention has been won by a rival picture or when the picture has never been anything other than an empty convention in his life. In each case, in one sense, the person remains familiar with the religious belief, but in another sense, the belief is meaningless for him. Kemp Smith has made a penetrating analysis of what often happens in such situations. He says that however these people

. . . may have thrown over the religious beliefs of the communities in which they have been nurtured, they still continue to be influenced by the phraseology of religious devotion – a phraseology which, in its endeavour to be concrete and universally intelligible, is at little pains to guard against the misunderstandings to which it may so easily give rise. As they insist upon, and even exaggerate, the merely literal meaning of this phraseology, the God in whom they have ceased to believe is a Being whom they picture in an utterly anthropomorphic fashion – a kind of Being who even if he were able to say to himself, 'All things are due to me' would still of necessity be pursued by the question, 'But whence then am I?' ([27] pp. 105–6)

Putting Kemp Smith's point in the terms used in this essay, one might say that the picture remains but divorced from its former use. Since the meaning of the picture is bound up with its use, any analysis of the picture in which its use is ignored and in which it is seen as a would-be empirical proposition, is bound to conclude that the picture is senseless. Of course, as far as Tolstoy's S. is concerned, the analysis would be a correct account of *his* belief, since it appears this is all his belief had ever been. This would not do for Nielsen's argument, however, since he is claiming that logical analysis can show the pictures to be mistaken even when they are seen by the non-believer to have the meaning which they have for believers. This is what I am denying.

A religious picture may be understood but lose its hold on a person's life in other circumstances. A tragic event in a person's life may make him unable to respond in the way the religious belief demands. Or a person may bring moral objections against the religious picture. In such circumstances, the religious picture may be called senseless, but it is important to recognise that this has little in common with demonstrating the falsity of an empirical proposition. The situation is far more akin to a radical moral disagreement, where one evaluative judgement is brought to bear against another. Again, a person may understand the force of a religious picture and yet not feel that he could live by it. He might feel great respect for those who can live by it. He might say, as Wittgenstein did once, that 'it is a document of a tendency in the human mind which I personally cannot help respecting deeply and I would not for my life ridicule it' ([41] p. 12).

One could go on enumerating different circumstances in which religious beliefs can be lost or partially lost. It would be important to note, if one were going into more detail, how there can be varying degrees in the hold religious beliefs have on people's lives. The line between belief and unbelief may not be at all sharp at many points, although this is not to say that the distinction between them can never be made. The above examples should be sufficient, however, to illustrate the point I am making, namely that it is not enough to point to the fact that people have rejected or lost religious beliefs to show that these beliefs are open to proof and disproof, weighing of evidence, etc., since it must still be shown that the kind of rejection and loss concerned are explicable in these terms.

It follows from what I have been saying that the man who has no use for the religious picture is not contradicting the believer. In his lectures on belief Wittgenstein brings out this point well:

Suppose someone is ill and he says: 'This is a punishment,' and I say: 'If I'm ill, I don't think of punishment at all.' If you say: 'Do you believe the opposite?' – you can call it believing the opposite, but it is entirely different from what we would normally call believing the opposite.

I think differently, in a different way. I say different things to myself. I have different pictures.

It is this way: if someone said: 'Wittgenstein, you don't take illness as punishment, so what do you believe?' – I'd say: 'I don't have any thoughts of punishment.' ([42] p. 55)

In discussing how religious pictures can lose their hold on people's lives, how pictures of immortality can decline, it is not enough to take account of such decline in the lives of individual believers. It is also necessary to note how religious pictures may decline because of changes in the culture to which they belong. In face of such decline one cannot ask, 'But whose fault is it that they are declining?' Consider the belief that marriages are made in heaven, and put alongside it the view which is often called 'realistic', namely, that relationships between men and women should be a matter of trial and error. If the latter idea is in the ascendancy, can we say that it is because the former conception has been shown to be mistaken? The parade of evidence which is supposed to establish this is likely to be itself based on the latter conception. Changes in the nature of family life which themselves have been brought by wider social change, for example, in conditions of work, have contributed to the decline of the belief that marriages are made in heaven. The belief has been isolated by the gradual disappearance of those social characteristics which nourished it. In time we find people saying, 'We just don't think like that any more', but that does not mean that the former conception was a mistake. Consider again the decline in the notion of family honour and the belief that one's personal desires should be subjected to it if they constitute the slightest threat to such honour. It is becoming increasingly hard to find people in our own society who would support such beliefs today. It is the easiest thing in the world, however, to find expressions of the view that parents have no right to stand in the way of their children, and that everyone has a right to lead his own life as he sees fit. But does this mean that the notion of family honour has been shown to be mistaken? In 'The Age of Innocence' Edith Wharton gives a beautiful portrayal of the decline in the notion of family honour in the fashionable society of New York in the 1870s. It is a story of how a man and woman subjected their desires to a certain conception of family honour and went their separate ways. At the end of the story, the man's son is shown to us as the beginnings of a new generation to whom such honour is unintelligible. The man, Newland Archer, reflects on the difference between the generations: 'The difference is that these young people take it for granted that they're going to get whatsoever they want, and that we almost always took if for granted that we shouldn't' ([36] pp. 280–1). What Edith Wharton gives us is a detailed picture of the shifting emphasis on the self and how this was brought about by subtle, but far-reaching social changes. One might call either emphasis deep, important, shallow or trivial. What I am saying is that it is not at all clear what would be meant by calling either emphasis a mistake.

I have considered the above example to illustrate that the kind of loss of belief or decline of religious pictures we have been talking of are not confined to religion. When such moral or religious pictures do decline, there is often no substitute for them. This is why the role of such pictures is trivialised if one considers them to be mere stories which serve as psychological aids in adhering to moral truths whose intelligibility is independent of them (cf. [2]). This is to speak as if the pictures were something people could use or dispose of at will, according to whether they served their purpose. It is also to speak as if one had a notion of truth apart from the pictures, by appeal to which they are measured. I have been stressing, however, that for the believer, it is the pictures that measured them. Wittgenstein stressed in his lectures that 'The whole *weight* may be in the picture' ([42] p. 72). The picture is not a picturesque way of saying something else. It says what it says; and when the picture dies, something dies with it, and there can be no substitute for that which dies with the picture.

This brings me to the last objection I want to consider against the arguments in this chapter. (4) Someone might suggest that if I am prepared to allow the possibility of the religious pictures dying, not simply in the life of a given individual, but in the life of a whole culture, should I not be prepared to say, on my suppositions, that there is a possibility of God dying? If certain moral modes of conduct were to pass away, some people might want to say that there is no goodness in the world any more. Why, then, would religious believers not want to say that if pictures of immortality were to die, God dies, as it were, with the pictures? I think the answer is that religious believers can say something now, from within the picture, about such a time of radical absence of belief. What they say is not that God has died, but that in such a time, people have turned their backs on God.

Of course it may be true, and probably is true, that at the moment, only a small number of people derive sustenance from the pictures of immortality we have been discussing. It is no doubt true that they are being replaced by new pictures which express different values. If one looks at the pictures of immortality which once were strong from the point of view of the lives people lead now in our society, what they consider to be important, and what they are afraid of, there may be good reason to describe the future by an ironic use of the words of St John and say that we see 'a new heaven and a new earth . . . for the former things are passed away'.

Notes

Chapter 1

1. Numbers in square brackets refer to sources listed in the Bibliography.

2. Of course, there is so-called evidence based on what are claimed to be messages from the dead. These 'messages' are sometimes supported by claiming that 'only so-and-so could have known that'. But Geach comments rightly that 'our ordinary beliefs as to what "only so-and-so can have known" are based on well-founded generalisations as to the limits of human knowledge. Regarding cases that would constitute exceptions to such generalisations, it is absurdly inconsistent to make inferences still using a premise that "only so-and-so can have known that". There is a well-known story in psychical research that ought to show the fallacy of such inferences. A medium gave a sitter touching and convincing "messages" as from the spirit of a dead friend, including things that "only he can have known"; but the friend turned out to have been alive and in a normal state of mind at the time of the "messages" ' ([9] p. 15).

3. In making this distinction and for many of the examples employed I am indebted to discussions with Mr Rush Rhees.

4. This is not strictly true. Robert Herbert imagines a situation, in which, after the death of a famous conductor, the dead man's musical ability, memories, temperament, etc., are found to be possessed by the chauffeur. The dead man's son and intimate acquaintances react to the chauffeur, after an initial bewilderment, in the ways they used to react to the dead father. Indeed, they say he *is* the father. The chauffeur says he is the famous conductor, and is as amazed at the state he finds himself in as other people are. To say that the chauffeur is simply exactly similar to the father is to misrepresent the reaction of the son and acquaintances. They say, 'He *is* the father.' Herbert says that recognising the form of life in which they say this does not mean that we must participate in it. 'It means that *as philosophers* we must see the

79

form of life as a "proto-phenomenon" and say, "This language-games is played" ' ([II] p. 87).

Even so, the kind of example envisaged by Herbert does not take us far when we are considering survival after death construed as survival in a life other than the one we are acquainted with as human beings. The identification of 'the chauffeur' with the father depends on the presence of characteristics which have their meaning in certain family and artistic traditions, and there is no suggestion that these belong to a world other than our own. (See pp. 16–17.)

5. I mean 'entirely unconnected' here to include the considerations I mention on pp. 16–17.

6. But see Chapter 4.

Chapter 2

1. This material appears in a somewhat extended form in [19].

Chapter 3

1. See pp. 12 f.

2. I am not suggesting that the deaths of *other* people can be adequately understood in terms of what the clinician has to say. This matter is too complex to pursue here. I'm simply noting that after all is said, there remain important differences between 'my death' and 'the deaths of others'.

3. I am indebted for these references to [1].

4. We shall have occasion to return to this point in the next chapter: see pp. 68–9.

Chapter 4

1. I owe this observation to Mr D. M. Evans.

2. See p. 58.

3. See p. 62.

4. This objection was put to me by Professor J. R. Jones in [12].

Bibliography

[1] Eugene I. Van Antwerp, 'An abstract of a Dissertation on St Augustine's 'The Divination of Demons and Care of the Dead' (Catholic University of America Press, Washington D.C., 1955).

[2] R. B. Braithwaite, 'An Empiricist's View of the Nature of Religious Belief' (Cambridge University Press, 1955).

[3] Charles Dickens, 'A Christmas Carol,' in 'Christmas Books' (Collins, London and New York, 1954).

[4] A. G. N. Flew, 'Death', in 'New Essays in Philosophical Theology', ed. A. MacIntyre and A. G. N. Flew (S.C.M. Press, London, 1955).

[5] A. G. N. Flew, 'Theology and Falsification', in 'New Essays in Philosophical Theology'.

[6] A. G. N. Flew, 'Locke and the Problem of Personal Identity', in 'Philosophy' (1951).

[7] A. G. N. Flew, 'Can A Man Witness His Own Funeral?', in 'Hibbert Journal', liv (1955–6).

[8] Philippa Foot, 'Moral Beliefs', in 'Proceedings of the Aristotelian Society' (1958).

[9] Peter Geach, 'Immortality', in 'God and the Soul' (Routledge & Kegan Paul, London, 1969).

[10] Peter Geach, 'The Moral Law and the Law of God', in 'God and the Soul'.

[11] Robert Herbert, 'Puzzle Cases and Earthquakes', in 'Analysis', xxviii (1967–8).

[12] J. R. Jones and D. Z. Phillips, 'Belief and Loss of Belief', in 'Sophia' (April 1970).

[13] Søren Kierkegaard, 'Purity of Heart', trans. Douglas Steere (Fontana Books, London 1961).

[14] D. M. MacKinnon, 'Death', in 'New Essays in Philosophical Theology'.

[15] Iris Murdoch, 'The Idea of Perfection', in 'Yale Review', liii (1963–4).

[16] Kai Nielsen, 'Wittgensteinian Fideism', in 'Philosophy', xlii (1967).

[17] D. Z. Phillips, 'Does It Pay To Be Good?', in 'Proceedings of the Aristotelian Society (1964–5).

[18] D. Z. Phillips, 'The Concept of Prayer' (Routledge & Kegan Paul, London, 1965).

[19] D. Z. Phillips and H. O. Mounce, 'Moral Practices' (Routledge & Kegan Paul, London, 1970).

[20] Plato, 'The Gorgias', trans. B. Jowett, 'The Dialogues of Plato', vol. ii (Oxford University Press).

[21] Plato, 'The Phaedo', in 'The Last Days of Socrates' (Penguin Classics, London, 1961).

[22] W. H. Poteat, 'Birth, Suicide and the Doctrine of Creation: An Exploration of Analogies', in 'Religon and Understanding', ed. and intro. D. Z. Phillips (Blackwell, Oxford, 1967).

[23] W. H. Poteat, 'I Will Die', in 'Religion and Understanding'.

[24] Rush Rhees, 'Art and Philosophy', in 'Without Answers' (Routledge & Kegan Paul, London, 1969).

[25] Rush Rhees, 'Natural Theology', in 'Without Answers'.

[26] Rush Rhees, 'Religion and Language', in 'Without Answers'.

[27] Norman Kemp Smith, 'Is Divine Existence Credible?', in 'Religion and Understanding'.

[28] J. L. Stocks, 'Morality and Purpose,' ed. and intro. D. Z. Phillips (Routledge & Kegan Paul, London, 1969).

[29] Stewart R. Sutherland, 'Immortality and Resurrection', in 'Religious Studies', iii (1967–8).

[30] Leo Tolstoy, 'Father Sergius', in 'The Kreutzer Sonata and Other Tales' (Oxford University Press, 1960).

[31] Leo Tolstoy, 'The Death of Ivan Ilych,' in 'The Works of Leo Tolstoy', vol. xv (Oxford University Press, 1934).

[32] Leo Tolstoy, 'A Confession in A Confession, The Gospel in Brief and What I Believe', trans. Aylmer Maude (Oxford University Press, 1954).

[33] E. B. Tylor, 'Primitive Culture' (Murray, London, 1920).

[34] Simone Weil, 'Concerning the "Our Father" ', in 'Waiting on God' (Routledge & Kegan Paul, London, 1951).

[35] Simone Weil, 'Gravity and Grace' (Routledge & Kegan Paul, London, 1963).

[36] Edith Wharton, 'The Age of Innocence' (Lehmann, London, 1953).

[37] B. A. O. Williams, 'Personal Identity and Individuation', in 'Proceedings of the Aristotelian Society', lvii (1956–7).

[38] Peter Winch, 'Moral Integrity' (Blackwell, Oxford, 1968).

[39] John Wisdom, 'Gods', in 'Philosophy and Psychoanalysis' (Blackwell, Oxford, 1952).

[40] Ludwig Wittgenstein, 'Tractatus Logico-Philosophicus', trans. D. F. Pears and B. F. McGuinness (Routledge & Kegan Paul, London, 1961).

[41] Ludwig Wittgenstien, 'A Lecture on Ethics', 'Philosophical Review', lxxiv (1965).

[42] Ludwig Wittgenstein, 'Lectures and Conversations on Aesthetics, Psychology and Religious Belief', ed. Cyril Barrett (Blackwell, Oxford, 1966).

[43] Ludwig Wittgenstein, 'Bermerkungen über Frazers "The Golden Bough" ', in 'Synthese' (Sept 1967).